# THE CHILD'S BOOK OF NATURE: ANIMALS

# The Child's Book of Nature: Animals

WORTHINGTON HOOKER

LIVING BOOK
PRESS

This edition published 2019
By Living Book Press

Copyright © Living Book Press, 2019

ISBN: 978-1-925729-90-0

NATIONAL
LIBRARY
OF AUSTRALIA

A catalogue record for this
book is available from the
National Library of Australia

# CONTENTS

# PREFACE.

HAVING PRESENTED in Part First such facts or phenomena of Vegetable Physiology as would be interesting to a child, I proceed in this Part to do the same with Animal Physiology.

The teacher and parent will observe, that in doing this I bring out quite prominently the analogies that exist between the animal and the vegetable world in the operations of life. Such analogies are always interesting to the child as well as to the adult, and the consideration of them adds much to the enjoyment of the observer of nature, for it opens to him the simple plans and principles upon which the Creator works out the almost endlessly varied results that life, both animal and vegetable, presents to our view.

What is true of the analogies that exist between the two kingdoms of life is also true of those that we find in each kingdom by itself. I have therefore, in this Part, traced the resemblances which the contrivances in the human system bear to those which we see in animals of different kinds, and also the differences, giving to some extent the reasons for them—that is, I have made it in some measure a book of comparative physiology. The effect of this mode of treating the subject will be to interest the child's mind in the observation of the various animals, great and small, that he sees from day to day. Natural History, which is otherwise rather a dull study, will thus become very attractive to him. And, to further this object, which I deem to be of great importance, I have noticed the habits of some animals in such a manner as to connect distinctly Physiology with Natural History, a relation which, though an obvious one, has very generally been disregarded.

While I have aimed in this Part at the same kind of simplicity as in the First, there are some points in it which require a greater compass of mind to understand. This is as it should be; for in going through the First Part there will, of course, be acquired by the learner some amount of skill in observation and reasoning. I have taken special care, however, not to presume too much upon the mental advance thus made.

WORTHINGTON HOOKER.

## CHAPTER I

## WHAT IS MADE FROM THE BLOOD.

I HAVE told you, in Part First, how every thing in a plant or tree is made from the sap. This is, then, the building material, as we may say, of the plant. Now every thing in your body is made from the blood. The blood, then, is to your body what sap is to a plant. It is the common building material of the body.

You remember what I told you in Part First about the full-blown rose. This is made from the sap that comes to the bud through the pipes in the stem. Just so the little finger of the child becomes the large finger of the man, from the blood that comes to it through the pipes in the arm. And as the stem of the plant grows larger all the time, so does the arm of a child. The sap makes the stem grow, and the blood makes the arm grow.

If you cut off a branch of a plant it stops growing, because the sap does not come to it any longer. It soon dies and decays. So, if the arm of a child be cut off, it can not grow, because no more blood can come to it. Like the cut-off branch, it dies and decays.

You see a twig come up out of the ground. It grows larger and larger every year. Soon it is a small tree. After many years it becomes very large, and spreads out its long branches over a great space. As you look up into it, you think of all that you see, its branches and leaves, as having been made from the sap that is continually running in its pipes. Now, as the little twig becomes a tree, so the infant in the cradle becomes the large man. And when you look up at a man, you can think of all his body as having been made from the blood that runs every where in its pipes, just as you think of a tree as made from the sap.

It is wonderful, as you have seen in Part First, how many and how different things are sometimes made from the same sap. Look at an apple-tree. There are the hard wood, the rough bark, the tender leaves, the beautiful blossoms, and the pleasant fruit, all made from the same sap. But the variety of things made from your blood is much more wonderful.

Look at some of the things that are made from the blood. See the skin, the hair, the nails. Look at the soft red gums and the hard white teeth in the mouth. Then look at the eye. See the eyelids, the eyelashes, the firm, pearly-white coat of the eyeball, and the clear window in the front part of the eye. See, too, inside of this window, that round, colored curtain, with an opening in the middle that we call the pupil.

All these different things that you see are made from the same blood. Then there are many other things inside of the body that you can not see. These are the hard bones, the red muscles, the white, shining cords by which the muscles pull the bones, the light, spongy lungs, the thick and firm liver, the soft brain, the white nerves, etc., etc.

How strange it is that all these parts of the body, so different from each other, are made from the same building material, the blood. But this is not all. The wax in your ears is made from the blood. So is the bile, that bitter stuff that is manufactured in the liver. The tears, too, are made from the blood. There are many other liquids in the body that are made from this common material. When you look into a person's eye you look into a watery fluid, and the back part of the ball of the eye is filled with a sort of jelly; both of these are made from the blood.

But even this is not all. The arteries and veins in which the blood runs are made from the blood. Even the heart that pumps the blood is made from the blood that it pumps. This is as strange as it would be to have the walls of a canal made from the water that runs in it, or to have a pump made from the water that it pumps out.

*Questions.*— What is every thing in a plant made from? What is every thing in your body made from? Tell what is said about the bud and the finger, and about the stem and the arm. What is said about cutting off a branch and an arm? How is a child compared to a twig? Mention the different things in an apple-tree that are made from the sap. Are there more things made from your blood? Mention some of them that you can see. Mention some that are inside of the body that you can not see. What is said about the ear-wax, the bile, the tears, etc.? What about the arteries and veins, and the heart?

## CHAPTER II.

## MORE ABOUT WHAT IS MADE FROM THE BLOOD.

HOW DIFFERENT from each other are some of the things that are made from the blood! You could hardly believe that the white, hard teeth are made from the same blood that the red, soft gums are. Suppose that while you are in a China-ware factory a man should tell you that even the whitest China is made from a red liquid, and that they also make in this factory fine red cloth from this liquid. You would not believe him. But white China-ware and the fine red cloth are not any more unlike than the teeth and the gums.

Suppose, now, that he should show you a yellow, bitter fluid, and then a clear, soft eye-water, and tell you that these he makes from the same red liquid from which the China and the red cloth are made. This certainly you would not believe. And yet, in our bodies, the bile and the tears are made from the same blood with the teeth and the gums.

But not only are a few things very much unlike made from the blood, but many things that differ from each other, some of them much and some but little. Suppose that the China-ware maker should tell you that besides making white China and red cloth from his red liquid, he made also a variety of both hard and soft things, such as velvet, and various kinds of cloth, nails, glass, etc. Impossible! you would say. But this is no more wonderful than that hair, teeth, gums, nails, bones, and all the different parts of the body should be made from that red fluid—the blood.

But suppose, again, that the China-ware man should tell you that his factory was made from the same red fluid from which he manufactures so many things in it—that the very pipes that carry the fluid around the building were made from it, and so also was the pump that sends it through these pipes. This would seem to you strangest of all. And yet all the various machinery of the body is made from the blood. The liver, that manufactures bile from blood, is itself made from blood; and so of other things; even the pipes in which the blood runs all over your body, and the heart that pumps it into them, are made, as I have before told you, from the blood.

The body is the house or habitation of the soul. It is a well-built and a well-finished house. The bones are its timbers. The skin is its covering. The hair is its thatched roof. The eyes are its windows. It is a house that can be easily moved about, just as the soul wishes. There is for this a great deal of machinery in it. And the soul has little cords, called nerves, running to all parts of this machinery, like telegraphic wires. There are also other kinds of machinery, as the breathing machinery, the machinery for taking care of the food, and the machinery for circulating the blood. The soul resides in the top of this house, the brain. Here it sends out messages every where by the little cords, and receives messages by them. Here it thinks and acts, and some of the time sleeps. This part of the house is very curiously and beautifully fitted up.

Now all the various parts of this house are made, as I have told you, from the blood, and yet there is more variety in them than there is in the parts and furniture of the houses that man builds. Suppose that a man should show you a great quantity of a red liquid, and tell you that with that he intended to build a house and furnish it—that he should make from it all his stones, and bricks, and timbers, and glass, and nails, and plaster, and papers for his walls, and paints of different colors, and then his carpets, and mirrors, and chairs, and curtains, etc., etc. You would say that the man is crazy. But God makes from that red fluid, the blood, all the parts of the house of the soul.

Exactly in what way all the different parts of the body are made from the blood we do not know. Wise men have studied this a great deal, and they have found out some things about it. What they have found out you are not yet old enough to understand. After all, the wisest men know but little about it, and, with all their wisdom, they do not know enough to make skin, or hair, or any thing else that you see in your body from the blood any more than, as I told you in Part First, they can make even a simple leaf from the sap.

*Questions.*— What is said about the teeth and the gums? Give the comparison about China and cloth. What is said about the tears and the bile? What is said about the variety of things made from the blood? Give the comparison about the China-ware factory and the machinery of the body. What is said about the different parts of the habitation of the soul? In what part of this house does the soul reside? Give the comparison about a house and its furniture. What is said about wise men?

## CHAPTER III

## HOW THE BLOOD IS MADE.

I HAVE told you what is made from the blood, and now you will want to know how the blood itself is made.

The blood in your body is made from the food that you eat. It is made very much in the same way that the sap in the plant is made. This sounds strange to you, but it is true. You remember that I told you in Part First that the plant's food is in the ground, and that the root is its stomach. You remember what I told you about the little mouths in the root that suck up the plant's food out of the ground. There are little mouths in your stomach that suck in the nourishing part of the food that you eat, as the mouths in the root suck up the nourishing part of the earth. And the stomachs of all animals have these little mouths.

The mouths in the root of a plant do not, you know, suck up all the soil. They drink in only what is good to make the plant grow. So the mouths in the stomach of an animal do not suck up all the food; they suck up only that part of the food that will make the animal grow—that is, what will make good blood. There is, you know, no sap in the ground, but there is what can be made into sap. So there is no blood in your food, but there is in it what can be made into blood. It is the business of the mouths in the root to take in what will make sap, and so it is the business of the mouths in the stomach to take in what will make blood. And they generally do this business very faithfully. It is very seldom that they take in what they ought not to.

You have seen how many different things are made from the blood. This is very wonderful. But it is quite as wonderful that the blood can be made from so many different kinds of food as you sometimes take into your stomach. Just think of all the various things that you sometimes eat at dinner—meat, potato, turnip, squash, apple-sauce, cranberry, celery, pie, filberts, raisins, etc. It seems strange that red blood can be made from such a mixture as this. But so it is. There is something in all these different things that helps to make the blood.

The blood is made from different things in different animals. The cow, you know, never eats meat. It would be of no use in its stomach. The mouths there would not suck up any thing from it. This is not their business. Their business is to suck up something from grass, and meal, and potatoes, etc., but not from meat. So grass would be of no use to a dog. The Creator has made the stomach of the cow in such a way that it can get from grass what is needed to make blood; and he has given such a stomach to a dog that blood can be made from the meat that he eats. Our stomachs are made in such a way that our blood can be made from a great many different things; and so the variety of our food is much greater than that of such animals as the cow and the dog.

*Questions.*— From what is the blood made? How is an animal's stomach like the root of a plant? What part of the food do the mouths in stomachs and in roots suck up? What is said about the different kinds of food that blood is made from? Tell about the food of the cow and the dog. What is said about our stomachs?

## CHAPTER IV

## MOTHER EARTH.

THE FOOD of plants is in the ground, and the roots take it up; but so, too, is the food of animals in the ground. And yet, if we should fill our stomachs ever so full of earth, we should not be nourished. How is this? It is because the food is not in the right condition for us while it is in the earth. It must be *changed* before our stomachs can do any thing with it.

Now this is just what the plants do for us. They get this food out of the earth for us, and put it into such a condition that our stomachs can use it. I will make this plain to you. We eat bread made from wheat. It nourishes us—that is, blood is made from it. But what is the wheat? It is grain that is made from the sap that comes up in the pipes of the stalk, and this sap is made from what the root sucks up out of the ground. You see, then, that what the wheat is made from is in the ground; and all that the plant does is to take this up out of the ground and make it into wheat, so that our stomachs can use it for food. The plant's stomach, then, we may say, gathers food out of the ground for our stomachs.

One of the things that we eat is sugar. Where does it come from? It is made from the earth. But if you should put earth into your stomach, no sugar could be made from it in your body. There are some plants that have to do this for us. They make sugar from the earth for us to eat. This part of our food then, may be said to be really in the ground, for what it is made from is there.

The same thing is true when you eat meat. This meat

was once a part of the ground. See how this is. Suppose it is a piece of beef from an ox: the grass that the ox ate was made from sap sucked up from the ground; then from this grass blood was made in the ox; from this blood the meat was made; and now from the meat blood is made to nourish you.

See, now, how many changes the food in the ground goes through in this case before it becomes a part of your body. First it becomes sap; then it becomes a part of the grass; then in the stomach of the ox it is sucked up, and is changed into blood; then it becomes a part of the ox; then it is sucked up in your stomach, and is changed into blood; and now it is ready to be used in your body to make nerve, or bone, or eye, or tooth, or any part of the house of your soul.

You sometimes drink the milk of the cow. This also comes from the ground. See how this is. The cow goes to pasture, and eats the grass that is made from the ground. The cow's blood is made from this, then milk is made in her bag from the blood, and in you this milk is changed back to blood.

So you see that all our food really comes from the earth. There is in the earth under our feet just what makes and nourishes our bodies. We can not get at it ourselves, mixed up as it is with the earth, but the plants suck it up and prepare it for us; and in this you see the reason for the expression "Mother Earth." The earth is our mother. We get all our food from the earth as really as the infant gets its food from its mother's breast.

You can also see, from what I have told you in this chapter, the meaning of the text, "Dust thou art, and unto dust shalt thou return." We are dust, that is, earth; for we are made from it, and are nourished by what comes from it, and when we die our bodies will become a part of the earth again.

You see that there are two reasons why animals have a stomach to put their food in. One is that they want to move about. They could not have a root for a stomach as plants do. They must have a stomach that they can carry about with them. We can suppose an animal made like a plant. It might have feet with roots sprouted out from them, and these roots might have little mouths which would suck up food as soon as they were put into the ground. But how very awkward and inconvenient this would be! The animal would be obliged every now and then to bury up its feet with their roots in loose moist earth, and stay still in one spot till enough was sucked up from the earth for its nourishment. And, besides, the roots would be dangling around, and catching in every thing as the animal moved about. Your little feet could not carry you about as nimbly as they now do if you had such roots fastened to them.

Another reason is, that the food in the ground is not fitted to nourish an animal. It must be gathered up in plants, and be changed in them, as I have shown you in this chapter, before it can be of any use to animals.

The stomach of a plant is much larger than that of an animal. The stomach of an animal, you know, is but a small part of its body; while the root of the plant—that is, its stomach—is nearly as large as the plant itself. What do you think is the reason of this? The little mouths in the root of the plant suck up only a small part of the earth, the plant's food, and so it takes a great deal of earth to give the plant all the sap that it needs. It is for this reason that the root spreads out so far on every side. Now in the animal the mouths in the stomach suck up a great part of the food. It does not require, therefore, a large stomach, for it needs to put but a small amount of food into it. You see, then, that the food of the plant is bulky, as we say, and therefore it must have a large stomach, while the animal can manage its food with a small one.

*Questions.*— Where is the food of animals? What must be done to it before they can use it? What do the plants do for us? Tell about the wheat. What is said about sugar? What about meat? Mention the changes that food goes through in this case before it becomes a part of your body. What is said of milk? What is the reason of the expression Mother Earth? Explain the text, "Dust thou art, and unto dust shalt thou return." What is the first reason given why an animal has a stomach to put his food in? What is the second reason? Why is the stomach of a plant so much larger than the stomach of an animal?

CHAPTER V.

## THE STOMACH AND THE TEETH.

THE LITTLE mouths in the stomach, as I have told you, suck up from the food what is made into blood, but they do not do this as soon as the food is put into the stomach. The food must be digested first. You have heard people talk about digestion, and now I will explain it to you.

When you swallow your food, there is a liquid formed in the stomach that mixes up with it. This liquid, after a little time, changes all the different kinds of food in such a way that the whole looks as if it was all one thing. The meat, and potato, and pie, etc., are not only well mixed, but they are so changed that you could not tell one from the other.

When the food becomes changed in this way, the little mouths begin their work upon it. They suck up from it a white fluid very much like milk; and it is from this fluid that all the blood in our bodies is made.

Now observe what is done to the food before it goes into the stomach. There is a mill in your mouth for grinding it up, and a very good mill it is. There are twenty teeth there for the purpose of dividing up your food very finely. You can see what the use of this is. The finer the food is, the more easily will the digesting fluid in the stomach change it. It takes some time for this fluid to soak through a solid piece of meat or potato. So you see that you must not swallow your food too fast, but must let the mill in your mouth grind it up thoroughly.

Something like this grinding we do sometimes for the

food of plants, You know that in the spring the gardener digs up his garden, and the farmer plows his fields. What is this for? It is to loosen up the ground; that is, it is to break up the food of the plants, so that they can use it well. If this was not done, the hard earth would be to the plants just as your food would be to your stomach if you swallow it without chewing it well. So your teeth do to your food what the spade and the plow do to the food of plants.

While the mill is grinding the food, there are some factories about the mouth, making and pouring forth a fluid to moisten it. This fluid, called the saliva, is what you feel in the mouth when the mouth waters, as we say. The two largest of these factories are just below your ears. It is these that swell up so much when one has the mumps. These saliva factories do a moderate business generally. Most of the time they only make enough liquid to keep the mouth moist. Sometimes they do not make enough even for this. This is the case when your mouth gets dry, as it is apt to do in fever. When you eat, these factories do a brisk business, for they then have to make a good deal of fluid to mix with the food. It seems as if they knew when it was necessary for them to go to work and make more saliva than usual. This, of course, is not so; but how it is that they are made to work so hard while we are eating we do not know.

The food of plants needs moistening just as our food does. The rain moistens it for the root, the stomach of the plant, so that it may get nourishment from it. When you water the dry earth in a flower-pot, you do for the food of the plant what the saliva factories do for your food.

Sometimes in fever, as I have just told you, the mouth is very dry. This is partly because the saliva factories have almost stopped work; hardly any saliva comes through their canals into the mouth. It would be hard work then to eat dry food. The dry cracker must be moistened before it can be eaten. This is very much like what sometimes happens to plants when there has been no rain for a long time. There they are, with their roots in the ground, just as they have been all along. The food is close to their little mouths, but it is so dry that they can not well manage it. They languish, therefore, and perhaps wilt. The dry earth is to them like the dry cracker to the fevered mouth.

*Questions.*— What is done to the food in the stomach? What do the months in the stomach suck up? What is done to the food before it goes into the stomach? What is the use of grinding the food? What harm does it do to eat fast? What is said about the food of plants? What else is done to our food while the teeth are grinding it? Tell about the working of the saliva factories. What is said about moistening the food of plants? How are plants sometimes like persons in a fever?

## CHAPTER VI

## MORE ABOUT THE TEETH.

NOTICE THAT in the mill in your mouth there are different kinds of teeth. They are for different purposes. The front teeth are for cutting the food; the large back teeth are for grinding it up fine; the pointed teeth, called the stomach and eye teeth, are for tearing the food.

You can see these different kinds of teeth in different animals. Every animal has such teeth as it needs to divide its food. The dog and the cat eat meat, and they want to tear this to pieces; they therefore have long, sharp, tearing teeth; so, too, have the lion and the tiger, for the same reason. Now look at the cow's mouth: she has no tearing teeth. The grass that she eats does not need to be torn; it needs to be bruised and ground up, and for this purpose she has large, broad, grinding teeth. These are her back teeth.

But you notice that the cow has a few different teeth in front; they are made to cut. Now watch a cow as she eats grass, and see how she uses these two kinds of teeth. With the front teeth she bites the grass—that is, she cuts it; then with the end of her tongue she puts it back where the grinding teeth are, to be ground before it goes into the stomach. So the cow has in her mouth both a cutting machine and a mill.

The horse has these two kinds of teeth, as you see represented in this figure, which is the skull of a horse.

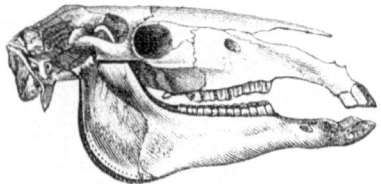

Now when you eat an

apple you do very much as the cow or the horse does with the grass; with your front cutting teeth you bite off a piece; then it is pushed back where the grinders are, and they grind it up into a soft pulp before you swallow it.

The cow does not always use her cutting teeth in the way that I have mentioned. See her as she eats hay; she does not cut this as she does the grass. With those front cutting teeth she merely takes up the hay, and it is gradually drawn back into the mouth, the grinders all the while keeping at work on it. If the hay is in a rack, she pulls it out with her cutting teeth. It is the same with the horse.

That beautiful and singular animal, the giraffe, which you see here, has these two kinds of teeth. This animal, when of full size, is three times the height of a tall man; it lives on the leaves of trees, which it crops with its front teeth, grinding them up with its large back teeth, as the cow and horse do their hay and grass.

You notice that your tearing teeth are not nearly as long and powerful as these teeth are in dogs, cats, tigers, etc. What is the reason of this? It is because, although you eat meat as they do, you can, with your knife and fork, cut up your food. They do not know enough to use such things, and so God has given them long, sharp teeth to tear their food to pieces.

The cow grinds the grass and hay twice. So do the sheep, the deer, the camel, the giraffe, and many other animals. See the cow cropping grass in the pasture; she grinds it partly in her mouth as she crops it, and then stows it away in a very large stomach that she has for the purpose; after a while she stops eating, and you see her standing or lying in the cool shade chewing her cud, as we say. That large stomach is very full of grass now, and this is all to be chewed over again. How do you think this is done? I will tell you.

After the grass is well soaked in this large stomach, it passes into another, for the cow has more than one stomach—she has four. In this second stomach the grass is all rolled into balls. This is a very curious operation. Now each one of these balls goes up into the mouth to be chewed over again. After it is well chewed, down it goes again, but it goes into still another stomach, and then up comes another ball to take its place; and so the cow goes on till all the balls are chewed. If you look at the cow's neck while she is doing this, you can see when the ball goes up and when it goes down. She seems to have the same quiet enjoyment while thus chewing her cud that the cat has when, with her eyes half open, she lies purring and wagging her tail after a full meal.

Birds, you know, have no teeth. Their mill for grinding food is not in the mouth, it is in the stomach. What we call the gizzard is this mill. See a hen pick up the corn that you throw to her. She swallows it very fast. Where do you think it goes to? It goes into a bag called the crop. Here it is soaked, just as the grass is in the large stomach of the cow. When it becomes soft enough it goes into the gizzard. Here it is crushed so as to make a soft pulp by being rubbed between two hard surfaces, as corn in a mill is ground between two mill-stones. If you cut open the gizzard of a fowl, you can see how well these surfaces are fitted to grind up the corn. They do it quite as well as teeth would. Birds that live on food that does not need grinding do not have a gizzard, but a common stomach.

*Questions.*— What are the different kinds of teeth that you have in your mouth, and what are they for? What is said about the teeth of the dog, cat, etc.? What is said about the cow's back teeth? What of her front ones? Tell how the cow uses these two kinds of teeth in eating grass, and how in eating hay. How do you eat an apple? Tell about the giraffe. Tell about the cow's chewing her cud. What is the crop of a bird for? What is the gizzard for? Do all birds have gizzards?

## CHAPTER VII

## THE CIRCULATION OF THE BLOOD.

YOU REMEMBER that I told you in Part First how the sap circulates in a plant or a tree. It goes up in one set of pipes, and goes down in another set. Just so it is with the blood in your body; it is always in motion. There are two different sets of pipes for it to go back and forth, as there are in the plant for the sap; these two sets of pipes are called arteries and veins.

The blood in your body is kept in motion by a pump that works all the time, night and day. This pump is in your chest. It is the heart. Put your ear to the chest of some one, and you can hear its working as it pumps out the blood. You can hear it in your own chest sometimes when it works very hard. When you have been running very fast you can hear it.

The heart pumps the blood out at every beat into a large artery. From this great main pipe other pipes or arteries branch out every where, and from these branches other branches go out; dividing in this way, like the branches of a tree, the arteries at last are very small.

At the ends of the arteries there are exceedingly small vessels. They are called capillaries, from the Latin word *capilla*, which means a hair. They are really smaller than the finest hairs, for you can not see them. When you cut your finger you divide a great many of these vessels, and the blood oozes out from them. When any one blushes, these capillaries in the skin of the face are very full of blood, and this causes the redness. It is the blood in these little vessels that makes the lips red. These capillaries are every where, so that wherever you prick with a pin the blood will ooze out.

The blood goes out from the heart by one set of pipes, and comes back to the heart by another set. It goes out from the heart by the arteries, as I have just told you; it comes back to the heart by the veins.

The veins lie, some of them, very deep, and some just under the skin. You see some of them under the skin in your arm and hand. But you can not see the arteries; they nearly all lie deep. Think of the reason of this. If an artery of any size is wounded, it is not easy to stop its bleeding, for the heart is pumping blood right through it; but it is easy to stop the bleeding of a wounded vein, because the blood is going in it quietly back to the heart. Now it is because it is so dangerous to wound arteries that God has placed them so deep that they can not easily be wounded.

The maker of our bodies has guarded the arteries in another way. He has made them much stronger than the veins. If they were not made very strong they would now and then burst. You sometimes see the hose of a fire-engine burst when they are working the engine very hard; but, though your heart pumps away sometimes so fast and hard, as when you have been running, not one of all the arteries gives way; but they would often burst if they were not made stronger than the veins are.

The blood in the arteries is red; but the blood that comes back to the heart in the veins is dark. This is the reason that the veins which you see under the skin look dark. I will tell you more about the dark and the red blood in the next chapter.

You see that the blood is kept in motion in a different way from what the sap is. In a large tree there is a great deal of sap going up in its trunk all the time, but there are no large pipes there like our arteries and veins. The sap goes up and down in a multitude of very small pipes, and there is no pump in the tree, as there is in our bodies, and in the bodies of other animals. How the sap goes up to the top of the tallest tree without being pumped up we do not know.

The heart is at work, as I have told you, all the time, while you are asleep as well as when you are awake. If it should stop pumping the blood, you would die. How steadily it works, going tick-tack all the while! How much work it does in a lifetime! It takes but a few days for it to beat a million of times; and here I will give you something about this work of the heart that I wrote in another book.[1]

If the heart could think, and know, and speak, suppose it should count up how many times it has to beat before the days of seventy years are numbered and finished. I think it would feel a little discouraged at the great, long work that was before it, just as some people do when they look forward and think how much they have to do; but remember that the heart has a moment in which it can make every beat. There is time enough to do the work; it is not expected to make two or more beats at once, but only one.

As the heart can not think, it does not faint with discouragement, but goes right on with its work, doing in each moment the duty of that moment; and it would be well if people that can think, whether children or adults, would take a lesson from this little busy worker in their bosoms. If one goes right on, performing cheerfully every duty as it comes along, he will do a great deal in a lifetime, and he will do it easily and pleasantly, if he does not keep

---

1     Every-day Wonders; or, Facts in Physiology. American Sunday-school Union.

looking ahead and thinking how much he has to do.

There is a pretty story, by Miss Jane Taylor, about a discontented pendulum. The pendulum of a clock in a farmer's kitchen, in thinking over the ticking that it had got to do, became discouraged, and concluded to stop. The hands on the clock-face did not like this, and had a talk with the pendulum about it. The pendulum was, after a while, persuaded to begin its work again, because it saw, as the hands said, that it always had a moment to do every tick in. The pendulum's foolish waste of time in complaining made the farmer's clock an hour too slow in the morning.

*Questions.*— What is said about the circulation of the sap and the blood? What is said about the heart? What about the arteries? What are the capillaries? By what pipes does the blood come back to the heart? Where can you see some of the veins? Why are the arteries laid deeper than these veins? Why are they made stronger than veins? What is the color of the blood in the arteries? What is its color in the veins? Is the sap kept in motion in the same way that the blood is? What is said about the work that the heart does? Tell about the pendulum.

## CHAPTER VIII

## BREATHING.

WHAT DO you breathe for? That is plain enough, you will say: I can not live without breathing. But why is it that your life depends on your breathing? This I will explain to you.

You remember that I told you that the blood that comes back to the heart in the veins is dark; it is not good blood. It has been used while it was in the capillaries in building and repairing bone, and skin, and muscle, and nerve, etc. It is not fit to be used again so long as it is dark blood. What shall be done with it? It must be made in some way into good red blood again. Now the factory where this is done is the lungs.

Just as fast as the dark blood comes to the heart, it sends it to the lungs to be made into red blood, then it goes back to the heart to be sent all over the body. But how, you will ask, is the dark blood changed into good red blood in the lungs? It is done by the air that you breathe in; every time that you draw a breath, air goes down into the lungs and changes the blood that it finds there.

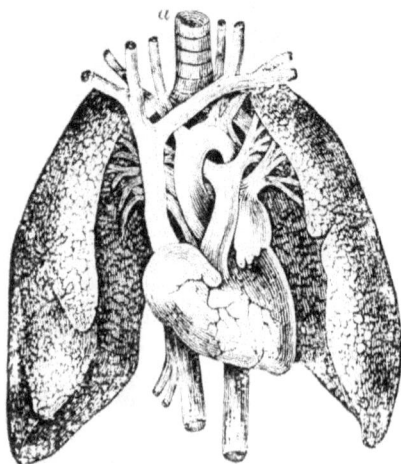

And now you see why it is that you have to breathe to keep alive. If the air does not go down into the lungs, the dark blood that is there is not changed into red blood: it goes back to the heart dark blood, and is sent all over the body; but this dark blood can not keep you alive: it is the red blood that does this.

You see, then, how death is caused in drowning; the air is shut out by the water, and the blood is not changed in the lungs; so the blood goes back to the heart dark instead of red, and is sent all over the body.

The heart and the lungs fill up your chest. The lungs cover up the heart, except a little part of it on the left side: this is where you can feel its beating so plainly. Here is a figure of the heart and lungs; the lungs are drawn apart, so that you can see the heart, and its large arteries and veins. You see, marked *a*, the windpipe by which the air goes down into the lungs. The lungs are light, spongy bodies. They are light because they are full of little cells for the air to go into. It is in these cells that the blood is changed by the air.

And now I will tell you about the lungs of fishes. But perhaps you will say that fishes do not breathe, and it can not be that they have lungs, for they would be of no use to them. It is true that they do not have such lungs as we have; but they have lungs, and they really do breathe air. How is this, you will ask, when they live in the water? There is a good deal of air always mixed up with water, and the lungs of a fish are so made that the air in the water can change the blood in them. The gills of a fish are its lungs, and the way that they are used is this. The fish takes water into its mouth, and lets it run out through the gills, and so the air that is mixed with the water changes the blood in them. Our lungs are fitted to breathe air alone, but the fish may be said to breathe air and water together. Air alone does the fish no good; he can not live in it; he must have his air mixed with water, or it is of no use to him.

Here is a picture of the lamprey eel. You see that it has a row of holes on its neck: these are openings that lead to its lungs; there are seven on each side. It is from this that it is sometimes called seven-eyes. Insects have such openings into their lungs. The grasshopper has twenty-four of them, in four rows. So you see that there are different ways of breathing in different animals. They do not all breathe through their mouths and noses, as we do.

You see that the chief use of breathing is to air the blood; but it is of use to us in another way. It makes the voice. We could not speak if we did not breathe. The sound of the voice is made in the top of the neck, in what we call Adam's apple. This is a sort of musical box at the top of the windpipe: in this box there are two flat cords stretching right across it. Now when we speak or sing, the sound is made in this way: the air, coming up out of the lungs, strikes on these cords, and makes them shake or vibrate. It is just as the vibration of the fiddle-string makes a sound when the bow is drawn over it. If you look at an Æolian harp fixed in a window, you can see that the strings are made to quiver by the wind, and this causes the sound. In the same way, the wind that is blown up from your lungs makes the cords in the Adam's apple vibrate; and the chest may be said to be the bellows of that little musical box or organ that you have in the throat.

Many animals have a musical box in the throat similar

to ours. The lowing of the cow, the barking of the dog, and the mewing and squalling of the cat are all done in such a box. You perhaps have wondered how the cat purrs. This noise is made in the same box where she does her mewing and squalling; for if you put your finger on her Adam's apple while she is so quietly purring, you can feel a quivering motion there.

Fishes, you know, have no voice. They have no musical box. If they had they could not use it, for the only way in which it can be used is to blow air through it. The frog can not use his so long as he is under water; he has to stick his head up out of water when he wants to croak.

*Questions.*— What do you breathe for? How is the blood in the lungs changed? What would it do if it were not changed? How is death, caused in drowning? How are the heart and lungs situated? Why are the lungs so light? What is said about the lungs of fishes? What is said about the breathing of the lamprey eel? What about the breathing of the grasshopper? How is the breathing of use besides changing the blood? Tell how the voice is made. What is said about the voices of animals? Where is the cat's purring done? Why do fishes have no musical box? What is said about the croaking of frogs?

## CHAPTER IX

## BRAIN AND NERVES.

I HAVE told you some things in the previous chapters about how the body is built and kept in repair. I have told you that the blood is the building material from which all the parts of the body are made. The use of food, you have seen, is to make the blood, and the chief use of the breathing is to keep the blood in good order. The heart, with its arteries and veins, keeps the blood moving all about the body, so that it may be used in building and repairing. But what is the body built and kept in repair for? It is a house for the mind or soul. The soul—the thinking part of you—so long as it remains in this world, dwells in the body.

The body is something more than a house for the soul. The head, where the soul dwells, is but a small part of the body. But it uses all parts of it. When the hand is moved, the soul uses the hand; when you walk, it uses the legs and the feet; when you see, it uses the eyes; it uses the ears as its instruments to hear with, and the nose is its smelling instrument; and so of other parts.

You can think, then, of the body as having in it many different kinds of machinery that the mind or soul uses. And the object of eating, and drinking, and breathing, and having the blood circulate, is to make all this machinery for the mind to use.

Let us see, now, how it is that the mind uses the machinery of the body. Raise your hand. What makes it go up? It is what we call the muscles. They pull upon it and raise it. But what makes them do it? They do it because you think to have them do it. It is your thinking mind, then, that makes them raise the arm.

But the mind is not there among the muscles; it is in your head. Now how does the mind get at the muscles to make them work? It does not go out of the brain to them, just as a man goes out of his house among his workmen to tell them what to do. The mind stays in the brain all the time; but there are white cords, called nerves, that go from the brain to all parts of the body, and the mind sends messages by these to the muscles, and they do what the mind tells them to do.

These nerves act like the wires of a telegraph. The brain is the mind's office, as we may call it; here the mind is, and it sends out messages by the nerves as messages are sent from a telegraphic office by its wires. This is done by electricity in the telegraphic office, but how the mind does it we do not know. When you move your arm, something goes from the brain along the nerves to the muscles, and makes them act, but what that something is we do not know.

If the wires that go out from a telegraphic office are broken off in any way, the man in the office may send out messages, but they will not go to the place he wishes. He may work his machine, and send the electricity along the wire, but it will stop where the break is. Just so, if the nerves that go to the muscles of your arm were cut, the muscles could not receive any message from the mind. You might think very hard about raising the arm, but the message that your mind sends to the muscles is stopped where the nerves are cut, just as the electricity stops where the break is in the wire.

While the mind sends out messages by one set of nerves, it receives messages by another set; it receives them from the senses. Just see how this is. If you put your finger upon any thing, how does the mind in your brain know how it feels? How does it know whether it is hard or soft, rough or smooth? The mind does not go from the head down into the finger to find out this; it knows it by the nervous cords that stretch from the brain to the finger. When you touch any thing, something goes, as quick as a flash, from the finger along these nerves to the brain where the mind lives, and lets it know what kind of a thing it is that your finger has touched. So, when you smell any thing, it is the nerves which connect your nose with the brain that tell the mind what kind of a smell it is. And when you taste any thing, it is the nerves of the mouth that tell the mind in the brain whether it is bitter, or sweet, or sour, etc. So, too, when you see any thing, it is the nerve which connects the eye with the brain that tells the mind what it is that you see.

The brain, in which the mind lives and with which it thinks, is the softest part of the body. You can see what sort of a thing your own brain is by looking at the brain of some animal at the meat-market. You can see it very well in the calf's head when it is prepared for cooking by being sawed in two. I have compared the nerves to the wires that stretch out from the telegraphic office; but there are only a few wires, while the nerves that branch out from the brain, all over your body, can not be counted. Here is a figure showing how the nerves branch out over the face and head; there are a great many of them, and so there are in all other parts of the body.

The nerves, by dividing, spread out, so that there are little nerves every where. If you prick yourself with a pin any where, there is a little nerve there that connects that spot with the brain, and that tells the mind about

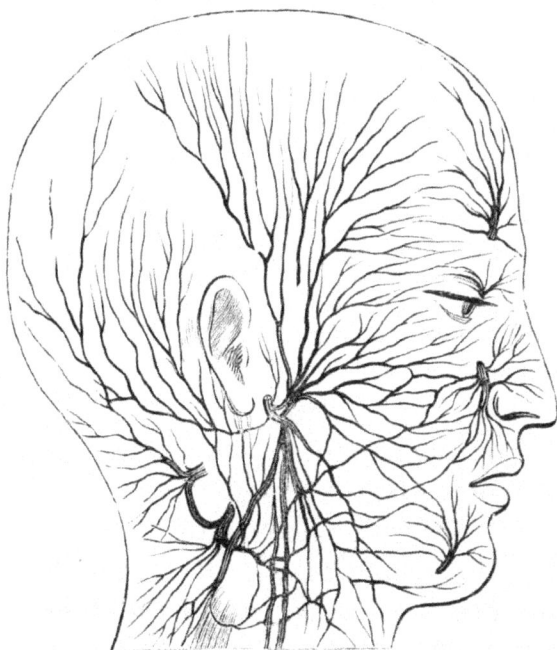

it. Now all the nerves in all parts of the body have their beginnings in the brain. In this soft organ are bundled together, as we may say, all the ends of the nerves, so that the mind can use them. There the mind is at its post, just like the man in the telegraph office; and from that great bundle of the ends of nerves it is constantly learning what is going on at the other ends of them in all parts of the body.

A great business the mind has to do in attending to all these ends of nerves in the brain; and how strange it is that it does not get confused, when so many messages are coming to it over its wires from every quarter! It always knows where a message comes from. It never mistakes a message from a finger for one from a toe, nor even a message from one finger for one from another.

And so, too, in sending out messages to the muscles,

there is no confusion. When you want to move a finger, your mind sends messages by the nerves to the muscles that do it. The message always goes to the right muscles. It does not go sometimes to the muscles of another finger by mistake, but you always move the finger which you wish to move. And so of all other parts. Messages go from your busy mind in the brain to any part that you move. You can see how wonderful this is, if you watch any one that is dancing or playing on an instrument, and think how the messages are all the time going by the nerves so quickly from the brain to the different parts of the body. I shall tell you more about this in another chapter.

The man in the telegraph office receives messages by the same wires by which he sends them out. It is not so, as I have told you before, with the mind's wires, the nerves; the mind receives messages from the senses by one set of nerves, and sends messages to the muscles by another set. If you burn your finger, you pull it away from the fire. Now in this case the mind gets a message from the finger by the nerves, and so knows of the hurt. The message goes from the finger along some nerves to their ends in that bundle of them in the brain; and the mind, being there on the watch, receives it. Now what does the mind do? Does it leave the finger to burn? No; it sends a message at once along some other nerves to the muscles that can pull the finger out of harm's way.

*Questions.*— What are some of the things that I have told you in the chapters before this? What is the body built and kept in repair for? In what part of the body does the soul live? Tell how it uses different parts of the body. When your arm is raised, how is it done? In what way does the mind make the muscles act? What are the nerves? How are they like telegraph wires? What is it that goes along the wires? Do we know what it is that goes along the nerves? Give the comparison between cut nerves and broken wires. From what does the mind receive messages? Tell about touching, smelling, tasting, and seeing. What is said about the brain? What is said about the number of nerves? What is said about the mind's attending to all its nerves? What is said about its making no mistakes in its messages? Give what is said about the burning of a finger.

## CHAPTER X

## HOW THE MIND GETS KNOWLEDGE.

THE MIND, as you learned in the last chapter, has a sort of telegraphic communication with all parts of the body by means of the nerves, and it is all the time receiving messages from the fingers, the eyes, the nose, the ears, the mouth, and other parts. These are instruments which the mind uses to get a knowledge of what is around us. It gets different kinds of knowledge by the different instruments. For example, it learns whether a thing is hard or soft by the touch of the fingers, and it learns how it smells by the nose, how it tastes by the mouth, and how it looks by the eyes.

There is knowledge, then, going all the time to the mind by the nerves from these instruments. It can not get there in any other way. Suppose the mind was locked up in the brain, and had no nerves going out from it. It could not learn any thing about what is around it; there might be eyes, and fingers, and ears, and a nose, and a mouth, but these would be of no use to the mind if there were no nerves.

See how the child learns about the world of things all around him. When he is first born he does not know any thing. He does not know how any thing feels, or looks, or tastes, or smells. But with his little nerves his mind gets messages from the senses, and so he learns every day about the things that are around him. Eyes, ears, nose, mouth, and fingers are all the time telling his mind something through the nerves. They tell him first about those things that are in the room where he is, and then, after a while, when he is carried out, they tell him about things that are out of doors, and thus he knows more and more every day.

And then, too, the mind thinks about what the senses tell it. It lays up what comes to it by the nerves, and looks it over, as we may say, and in this way it learns a great deal. There is great difference in people in this thinking about what the mind knows by the senses. Some that see and hear a great many things do not know as much as some that see and hear few things. It is because they do not think much about what the senses tell the mind.

You see, then, that all that we learn in this world really comes into the mind by the way of the nerves from the senses—the sight, the hearing, the touch, the smell, and the taste. The senses are the *inlets* or openings by which knowledge enters, and the nerves are the passages by which it gets to the mind in the brain; and after it gets there the mind thinks about it and uses it in various ways.

Some persons, you know, do not have all these inlets for knowledge open. For example, some are deaf; in them no knowledge can get into the mind by the ears. Some are blind, and no knowledge can get into their minds by the eyes. More knowledge comes into the mind by the sight than by the hearing; it is therefore a greater misfortune to be blind than it is to be deaf.

It is astonishing to see how much the deaf and the blind can learn if they try. If the mind is wide awake and ready to learn, it can get a great deal of knowledge even when one of the openings for it is shut up. It can use the knowledge gained by the other senses in such a way as to make up very much for the loss. A lazy mind, with all the senses letting in knowledge, will not know as much as a busy mind will with one of the senses shut up. In the deaf and dumb the eyes have to answer for both eyes and ears in getting knowledge. They have to do double duty; and they do it very well if the mind is only wide awake and attentive to all that it can learn by the eyes. In the blind the ears have to do a great deal more than in those that can see. The fingers also of the blind are very busy, for they learn very much about what is around them by the sense of feeling. There are books now made for their use with raised letters. By passing their fingers over them, they read just as you do by looking at printed letters.

And now I will tell you about a girl that has had to get all her knowledge with only one of the senses, the sense of feeling. Her name is Laura Bridgman. When she was in her second year she became very sick. Her sickness lasted a very long time. After she got well it was found that she was blind and deaf, and that she had no taste nor smell; only one of the five inlets for knowledge was open. All that could come into her mind was what could be learned by the touch alone. But she had an active mind, and so she went round feeling of every thing, to find out all she could about things.

The only way that she could know people was by feeling them. Her mother was very kind to her, and the little helpless girl liked to be with her all the time. She followed her about the house, and tried to do things just as her mother did them. She would feel of her mother's arms and hands while she was doing things, that she might find out how she did them. In this way she learned to knit, which was a great comfort to her, for she did not like to be idle.

A kind physician, who had charge of an asylum for the blind in Boston, heard about Laura. He was much interested for the helpless child, and went to see her.

He persuaded her mother to let her come to the asylum. Laura did not feel at home at first, but, as they were all kind to her in the asylum, she soon liked it very much.

She now began to learn many things, and I will tell you a little how the teacher managed with her. He put into her hands different things—spoons, keys, books, etc. Each article had a label on it. The letters on the labels were raised letters, such as are used in teaching the blind. She would feel them all over with the tips of her little fingers, her busy mind all the time thinking about how they felt. Then the labels and the things were put before her, but separated from each other. After a little trying, she learned to put the labels on the things right.

All this time she did not know that these labels had the names of the articles on them. If she were blind only, she would have known this at once, for she could have been told of it; but after a while she in some way got this idea into her mind. She was delighted, for she had now found a new way of learning things, and of telling about things to others.

And now Laura went on fast with her learning. The letters were separated, and she would put them together so as to spell spoon, key, etc. This was a great amusement to her. Sometimes, when she carelessly placed the letters wrong, she would playfully strike her right hand with her left one, and then, when the letters were placed right, she would pat her head, as the teacher was apt to do when he was pleased with any thing that she had done.

After a while the teacher taught Laura to use her fingers in talking, as you, perhaps, have seen the deaf and dumb do. She soon learned to make all the letters in this finger-alphabet, which you can see on page 98; and now she could talk with people quite easily, if they happened to know this alphabet. When she had any thing to say, she would make the letters with the fingers, while the person to whom she was talking would look at her. But how do you think that she managed when this person said any thing to her with his fingers? She could not see his fingers, but she could feel them, and this was the way in which she knew what was said to her; she would carefully, but rapidly, pass her fingers over his as fast as he made the letters. It was surprising to see how quickly the touch of her nimble fingers would tell her mind what letter was made, and how fast she could converse with persons in this way.

Laura learned much more at the asylum than we should suppose she could with only her one sense of touch. Some persons with the whole five senses do not know as much as she does. She even learned to write; and writing and knitting were very pleasant employments to her. By writing she could put the thoughts of her busy mind on paper, so that others might read them; and while she was sitting alone thinking, she liked to make her nimble fingers useful in knitting. It was a great satisfaction to her that, though she had but one sense, she could do something useful. What a pity it is that many children, and many adults too, do not have more of this feeling than they seem to have! The example of Laura teaches a good lesson to all idlers.

Though Laura could never see beautiful things, nor hear pleasant sounds, as you do all the time, she was very cheerful, and sometimes she was very funny. She liked to play with her doll; and as the blind children in the asylum had ribbons tied over their sightless eyes, she tied one over her doll's eyes. One day she was in her play taking care of her doll as one would of a sick child. She made believe give it medicine, and put a hot bottle to its feet; and when some one proposed to her to put a blister on its back, she was so much amused that she laughed and clapped her hands.

After Laura had been some time at the asylum her mother came to see her. She did not know her mother at first, but thought that she was some stranger. She held back and would not come near. Her mother handed her a string of beads which she used to wear when at home. She took them, and as soon as she felt them she knew what beads they were. She put them on her neck, and, showing great joy, said with her finger-language that she knew these came from home. Something else from home was given her. She now drew near, and her mother kissed her. The moment that her mother's lips touched her she knew who it was, for that kiss was just like the many kisses her loving mother used to give her. She remembered how those lips used to feel, and they had the same feeling now; and now she clung to her mother, and put her head into her bosom. They were both very happy. When her mother left her Laura felt sad indeed. She wanted to go with her, but she knew that it was best for her to stay in the asylum, where she could learn so much.

*Questions.*— What are the instruments by which the mind gets its knowledge? How does the knowledge get to the mind? What good would the instruments do if there were no nerves? Tell how the child, when first born, learns about things around him. What is said about thinking of what is learned by the senses? Why may the senses be called the inlets of knowledge? Tell about the deaf and the blind. Why is it worse to be blind than it is to be deaf? What is said about the amount of knowledge that the blind and the deaf can obtain? What is said about the sense of sight in the deaf and dumb? What senses do the blind chiefly use in getting knowledge?

How do they read? How many of the senses did Laura Bridgman lose? How did she learn about things before she went to the asylum? Tell how she learned after she went there. How did she talk with people? Tell about her industry. What is said of her cheerfulness? What of her fun? Tell About her mother's visit.

## CHAPTER XI

## SEEING.

THE SENSES by which the mind obtains most of its knowledge are the sight and the hearing. In this chapter we will look at the organ or instrument of sight.

The eye is a very beautiful instrument. It is very nicely made, and it has a great many different parts. You are not old enough yet to understand all about these parts, but there are some things about them that I can explain to you.

What we call the white of the eye is a strong, firm sort of bag. It is filled mostly with a jelly-like substance. It is this that makes it a firm ball. If it were empty it would be like a bag. Into the open part of this, in front, is fitted a clear window. The light goes in here. It can not get in at the sides of the eyeball, through the thick white of the eye.

Through this very clear window you can look into the bag or ball of the eye. You can not look through the jelly-like substance that is there, and see the very back of the inside of the eyeball; but it is like looking into a dark chamber. The reason that it is so dark is, that it is lined with something almost black. If this were not so, the eyes would be dazzled with the light that commonly goes into them, just as they now are when the light is very bright indeed.

Inside of the front window of the eye that I have told you about there is a fluid as clear as water. In this fluid you see a sort of curtain with a round opening in it. This opening is called the pupil of the eye. It is not always of the same size. When there is a very bright light, it is small; but when the light is dim, it is large, for then you want all the light that you can get in that dark chamber where the jelly is. You can see the pupil change in its size if you look into the eye of any one while you bring a light very near, and then move it off quickly.

The curtain in which this opening is we call the iris. It is circular. Its outer edge is fastened all round to the inside of the eyeball. The watery fluid, that I told you is inside of the window of the eye, is on both sides of this curtain. It would not do to have the jelly here, for the curtain would not move easily in that in changing the size of its opening.

The iris is, you know, of different colors in different persons. When it is blue, we say that the person has a blue eye; and if it is quite dark, we say that he has a black eye; and so of other colors. This curtain makes the eye very beautiful; but its chief use is, as you see, to regulate the quantity of light that goes into the eye. When there is a great deal of light, the curtain is drawn in such a way as to have the round opening very small; but when there is little light, it is drawn so as to make this opening large. This curtain must be made very nicely, or it would be puckered when the opening in it is changed in this way. No man could make a curtain of this shape, and have it work like this: it would be a very awkward thing if he should undertake it. He could not possibly make it so that the round opening in it could be made smaller and larger without wrinkling. But look at this beautiful curtain in the eye, and see how smooth it is, and how perfectly round its edge keeps, as the size of the pupil is changed. Did you ever see any thing work more prettily and easily than this does?

The opening in the curtain is different in different

animals. In the cat it is of this shape;

in the horse it is shaped in this way.

You can see the difference in the size of the cat's pupil in different lights: if you look at her eyes in a bright sunlight, and then again in the evening, you will see that it is very much larger in the evening than it is in the day. When the sun is very bright, her pupil is a mere

chink, like this; but in the evening it is very wide open,

shaped in this way.

But I have not yet told you how you see. It is done in this way. The light that goes in through the pupil makes an image or picture there of every thing that is before the eye. It makes the image on a very thin sheet spread out on the back part of the dark chamber where the jelly is; it is just as light makes images of things in a looking-glass, or in the smooth, still water; the only difference is, that the image or picture in the eye is very small. When you see a tree pictured in the still water, the picture is as large as the tree itself; but the picture that the light makes of the tree in that dark chamber of your eye is very small. The picture in your eye of a whole landscape, with all its trees, houses, hills, etc., does not cover over a space larger than a ten cent piece.

But how does the mind in the brain know any thing

about these pictures? It knows about them by means of a nerve, that goes from the brain to the eye, and is spread out where the pictures or images are made. It would do no good to have the pictures made in the eye, if the nerve could not tell the mind about them. The eye might be perfect, and yet there might not be any seeing. It is as necessary to have the nerve in good order as it is the eye itself. It is not your eye that sees; it is your mind, and in seeing it uses both the nerve and the eye.

You have two eyes. When you look at one thing, say a house, there is a picture of the house in both eyes. The two nerves tell the mind in the brain about the two pictures. How is this? Why does not the mind see two houses? It is because the pictures in the two eyes are exactly alike, and both nerves, therefore, tell exactly the same story; if they did not, then the mind would see two houses; that is, it would see double, as it is called. You can see double by pressing one eye sidewise while you let the other go free.

The eyes of insects are very curious. You remember what I told you about compound flowers. Now, as in a compound flower there are a great many flowers together, so it is with the eyes of insects. The eye of a common fly is made up of thousands of eyes; so, when he looks at any thing, there are thousands of very little images of it made by the light in these eyes, and the nerves tell the fly's mind, in his little brain, about them. These eyes are so exceedingly small that you can not see them without a microscope. How fine, then, must be the nerves that go from them to the fly's brain! Your eye is a very wonderful instrument, but God has put thousands of them just as wonderful into the head of the fly that buzzes about you. It is as easy for him to make little eyes as large ones, and he can make a multitude as easily as one.

*Questions.*— By what senses does the mind learn the most? What is the white of the eye? What is it filled with? What is there in the front part of the eye? What is said about the dark chamber of the eyeball? What is just inside of the front window of the eye? What is the pupil of the eye? What is the iris? How is it arranged? What is said of its color? What is its chief use? Tell about this. What is said about its being made nicely? What is said about the shape of its opening in different animals? What is said about the cat's pupil in different lights? Tell about the images made in the eye. What is said about the nerve of the eye? How is it that, with two eyes, you do not see double? Why do you have two eyes? What is said about the eyes of insects?

## CHAPTER XII

## HOW THE EYE IS GUARDED.

THE EYE, you know, is a very tender organ. It is therefore guarded thoroughly, and it is really very seldom hurt. But notice that it is just where it would be likely to be hurt if it were not thus guarded. It is right in the front part of the head. It must be there for the mind to use it in seeing. And it is much of the time open. You would suppose, then, that it must very often be struck and hit by things that are thrown about; but it is really very seldom hit so as to be hurt much.

The parts about the eye are often injured, but the eye itself generally escapes. We often see the eyelids and the cheek black and blue from a blow, and yet the tender and delicate eye is as sound as ever. People say, in such cases, that the eye is black and blue, but this is not so; the injury is all on the outside, and does not go into the eye.

Now let us see in what ways the eye is guarded. It is in a deep bony socket. There is bone all around it except in front. Then, too, see how the bones stand out all around it. The bone of the forehead juts over it. Below and to the outside stands out the cheek bone, and the nose is its wall on the inside. Now you can see that a blow with a stick would be very likely to strike upon some of these walls of bone, and the eye would then escape. They are real walls of defense to the eye. A stick can not hit the eye itself unless it goes with its end pointed to the eye. It must go in this way to avoid striking on these walls, or parapets of bone, by which the eye is surrounded.

But if the stick gets by these bony walls, it may not

hurt the eye, after all. Perhaps you never thought what use there is in being able to wink so quickly. See what winking does. It shuts the eyelids over the eye, so that nothing can get into it unless it is something sharp enough to pierce through the lids. And a blow will not hurt the eye, if the lids are closed, unless it is hard enough to bruise it through the lids.

How quick is the working of that winking muscle! The moment that the eye sees any thing coming toward it that may injure it, this muscle shuts up the eye out of sight as quick as a flash. It hardly seems as if there was time for a message to go from the eye to the brain, and then another back from the brain to that muscle in the lids. But all this happens. The nerve of the eye tells the mind of the danger, and the mind sends a message to the winking muscle. This is done so quickly that whenever people speak of any thing as being done very quickly, they are very apt to say that it was done in the twinkling of an eye. This expression is used in the Bible in this way.

But I have not told you all that this winking muscle does. It does something more than shut the eye in. It pushes it back in its socket, so that it is a little farther out of the way of a blow. And it does not push it right against the hard bone of the socket: there is a soft cushion of fat for it to press the eye against.

And this is not all. When the eye sees a blow coming, this muscle acts so strongly that it wrinkles the skin of the eyelids, and pulls down

the eyebrow, and draws up the cheek, as you see here.
Now see how this guards the eye. The cheek and the
eyebrow are brought so near together that there is but
little room for the blow to get at the eye; and even if it
does, the wrinkled skin of the lids makes a cushion over
it that breaks the force of the blow. You can see that the
blow would be much more apt to do harm if the winking
muscle merely brought the lids together. As it is, a blow
commonly hits on the eyebrow or cheek, or both, while
the eye is safe, shut up and pushed back in its cavern
upon its cushion of fat. To see how much the bringing
together of the cheek and eyebrow defends the eye, you
must look at some one as he forcibly closes the eye, as
represented in the figure. And if, at the same time, you
put your finger on the parts, you will see how the cushions
which all this wrinkling makes over the eye and about its
socket defend it from harm.

So you see that not only is the eye guarded by parapets
of bone, but the busy winking muscle raises up cushions
on them whenever the eye sees a blow coming. These
cushions often save the bone from being cracked, and in
this way also keep the eye from being hurt.

Of what use do you think the hairs on the eyebrows
are? They are for good looks, you will say. But they are
for something more than this; they are a defense to the
eye. How this is I will explain to you. You know what the
eaves of a house are for when there is no trough to the
roof; they keep the rain from running down from the
roof on the sides of the house. They make it drop off to
the ground a little way from the house. Just so the hairy
eyebrows make the sweat of the forehead drop off upon
the cheek, instead of running down into the eye. The eyebrows, then, are the eaves of the roof of the eye's house.

Perhaps you will ask what hurt the sweat would do if it should run down into the eye. It would be very disagreeable; and, besides this, it would irritate the eye and make it red. The eye would become inflamed.

The eyelashes, too, besides making the eye look well, are a defense to it. You know that there are often small things flying about in the air which we are not apt to see. If these fly against the eye, they generally hit against the eyelashes, and so are prevented from going into the eye.

The tears, also, are a defense to the eye. If any thing happens to get by the eyelashes into the eye, how quick the tears flow to wash it out! Commonly the gland, or tear factory, only makes enough tears to keep the eye a little moist; but as soon as any thing gets into the eye and irritates it, the tear factory sets to work briskly, and sends down the tears abundantly. At the same time, the winking muscle keeps moving the lids, and generally what is in the eye is soon washed out.

Tears are flowing into the eye all the time. If they did not, the eyeball and the inside of the lids would become dry, and they would not move easily on each other. You would have to keep wetting them with water to prevent them from rubbing. The tear factory, which is just above the eye, continually sends down, through some little tubes or ducts, just enough tears to make the motion of the eye and the lids easy.

But you will ask where the tears that are made go. They do not commonly run out over the lids, and they must go somewhere. I will tell you about this. If you look at the eyelids of any one, you can see in each lid a little hole at the end of the edge toward the nose. The tears go into these holes, and down through a duct that ends in the nose. This duct may be called the sink-drain of the eye, for the tears, after washing the eye, run off through it. The two little holes or mouths in the lids commonly take in all the tears as fast as they come to them; but when we cry, the tear factory makes tears so fast that these mouths can not take them all in. The tears, therefore, overflow their banks—the lids—and run down on the cheek.

*Questions.*— Is the eye in a very exposed situation? Why is it seldom much hurt? Are the parts about it often hurt? Tell how the bones about the eye defend it. Of what use is winking? What is said about the quickness with which it is done? What else does the winking muscle do besides shutting the eye? What does it push the eye back upon? What else does this muscle do besides what has been mentioned? How does this defend the eye? On what does a blow aimed at the eye commonly hit? Of what use are the hairs on the eyebrows? What harm would the sweat do if it ran down into the eye? Of what use are the eyelashes? In what ways do the tears prevent the eyes from being injured? Where do the tears go to from the eye? What happens when one cries?

## CHAPTER XIII

## HEARING.

WHAT IS sound? If you look at a large bell when it is struck, you can see a quivering or shaking in it. If you put your hand on it, you can feel the quivering. It is this that makes the sound that we hear. You can see the same thing in the strings of a piano when they are struck, and in the strings of a violin as the bow is drawn over them. The wind makes the music on the Æolian harp in the window by shaking its strings. And when you speak or sing, the sound is made, as I have told you before, by the quivering of two flat cords in your throat.

But when a bell is struck, how does the sound get to our ears? The quivering or vibration, as it is called, of the bell makes a vibration in the air, and this vibration is continued along through the air to our ears.

The vibration can go through other things besides the air. It will go through something solid better than it will through air. Put your ear at the end of a long log, and let some one scratch with a pin on the other end, you can hear it very plainly. The vibration made by the pin travels through the whole length of the log to your ear; but if you take away your ear from the log you can not hear it, for the vibration or sound can not come to you so far through the air.

The nearer you are to where the sound is made, the louder it is; and the farther sound goes, the fainter it is. It is said to die away as it goes; that is, the vibration becomes less and less, till, after a while, it is all lost. It is like this: if you drop a stone into water, it makes little waves or ripples in all directions. These become less and less the farther they go from where the stone was dropped. It is just so with the waves or vibrations of sound in the air.

What is an echo? It is when a sound that you make comes back to you again. It is done in this way. The vibration strikes against some rock, or house, or something else, and then bounds back to you, just as a wave striking against a rock bounds back.

Why is it that a person speaking in a building can be heard more easily than one speaking in the open air? It is because the vibrations are shut in by the walls. It is for the same reason that you can hear a whisper so far through a speaking tube extending from one part of a building to another. The vibrations are shut in within the tube. They have no chance to spread out in all directions, and they go right straight on through the tube.

I have thus told you how sound is made, and how it goes through the air and through other things; but how is it that we hear sound when it comes to our ears? How does the mind know any thing about the vibration of the air? This vibration does not go into the brain, where the mind is; it only goes a little way into the ear, and there it stops. It comes against the drum of the ear, and can go no farther. How, then, can the mind know any thing about it? This I will tell you.

The vibration of the air goes into the ear to a membrane fastened to a rim of bone, and called the drum, and shakes it, and this shakes a chain of little bones that are the other side of this drum-head. The last of these bones is fastened to another little drum, and, of course, this is shaken. This drum covers an opening to some winding passages in bone. These passages are filled with a watery fluid. Now the shaking of the second little drum makes this fluid shake. The nerve of hearing feels this shaking of the fluid, and tells the mind in the brain.

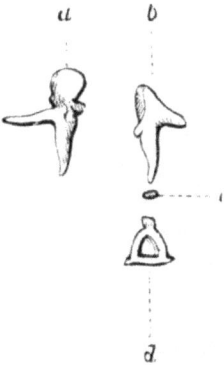

Here are the four little bones that make the chain of bones in the ear. They are curiously shaped. The one marked *a* is called the hammer, and *b* is called the anvil. The little bone marked *c* is the smallest bone in the body. That marked *d* is called the stirrup. This is the bone that is fastened to the second drum—the one that covers the opening into the winding passages. The vibration that comes to the first drum is passed on by this chain of bones to the second drum.

See, now, how many different shakings there are for every sound that you hear. First, the bell, or whatever it is that makes the sound, shakes. Then there is a shaking of the air. This shakes the drum of the ear. Then the chain of bones is shaken. The farthest one of them shakes another drum, and this shakes the fluid in the bony passages. All this happens every time that you hear a sound; and when you hear one sound after another coming very quickly, how the vibrations chase each other, as we may say, as they go into the ear! But they are not jumbled together. They do not overtake one another. Every vibration goes by itself, and so each sound is heard distinct from the others, unless the vibrations come very fast indeed. Then they make one continued sound. Each puff of a locomotive, when it starts, is heard by itself. The vibration of one puff gets into the fluid in the bony passages before the one that follows it; but as the locomotive goes on, the puffs get nearer and nearer together, and when it goes very fast, they are so near together that the vibrations do not go separate into the ear, and they make a continued sound.

Sound, I have told you, spreads in all directions in vibrations or waves. Now the more of these waves the ear can catch, the more distinct is the hearing. Some animals that need to hear very well have very large ears. Here is one, the long-eared bat. He must hear very well indeed, for his monstrous ears must catch a great many of the waves of sound. We could hear better if our ears were larger; but large ears would not look well on our heads; and we hear well enough commonly. Sometimes, when we do not hear as distinctly as we wish to, we put up the hand to the ear, as you see represented on the opposite page. This helps the hearing by stopping the waves of sound, and turning them into the ear. Those who are very deaf sometimes have an ear-trumpet, as it is called. In using it, the large trumpet end is turned toward the person speaking, so as to catch the vibrations, while the tube part of it is in the ear.

Some animals can turn their ears so as to hear well from different directions. How quickly the horse pricks up his ears when he sees or hears something that he wants to know more about; and then he can turn his ears backward when he wants to do so. It is in such timorous animals as the hare, the rabbit, and the deer, that we see the ears most movable. They are on the watch all the time for danger, and the least sound that they hear they turn their ears in the direction of it. Their ears, too, are large, so that they hear very easily.

I have told you how the eye is guarded. The ear is well guarded also. I do not mean its outer part: it is the inner parts, where the hearing is really done, that are so well guarded. You remember that I told you that there are passages filled with a fluid. The nerve of hearing has its fine, delicate fibres in these passages. They feel the shaking of the fluid, and tell the mind of it. Now it is necessary that this part of the hearing apparatus should be well guarded; for this reason, these passages are inclosed in the very hardest bone in the body.

Then, too, the very entrance into the ear is well guarded, and in a curious way. The pipe that leads into the drum of the ear is always open, and you know bugs are very apt to crawl into such holes. What do you suppose is the reason that they do not often crawl into the ear? There is something there to prevent them. It is the wax. They probably do not like the smell of it, and so, if they come to the entrance, they turn about. Once in a while one goes in, and then he is prevented from doing much harm by the wax. He is soon covered with this, and it is so sticky that it keeps him from kicking very hard. And, after all, though he may cause some pain, he can not get at the delicate part of the machinery of the ear. He dies after a while, if he is not got out, and perhaps the bitterness of the wax has something to do with killing him.

*Questions.—* How is sound made? How does it get to our ears? Tell about the vibration of sound in a log. What is said about the dying away of sound? What is this like? What is an echo? What is said about speaking in a building? What about speaking through a tube? Tell how we hear sound. Tell about the little bones in the ear. What do these bones do? Tell what the different vibrations are in hearing. What is said about the puffing of a locomotive? Why do some animals have large ears? Why are our ears so small? What animals can turn their ears different ways, and why? How is the inner part of the ear guarded? Tell what is said about the wax.

## CHAPTER XIV

## THE SMELL, THE TASTE, AND THE TOUCH.

I HAVE told you that most of what the mind knows about the world around it comes to it by the sight and the hearing. But it learns a great deal by the other senses, and these I will tell you about in this chapter.

Did you ever think how it is that you smell any thing? You put a rose up to your nose, and the fragrance is pleasant to you. Now what is this fragrance? Is it something that goes up into your nose? You can not see any thing come from the rose. But in reality very fine particles come from it. They are finer than the finest powder. They float every where about in the air, and, as you breathe, they go with the air into your nostrils. Every perfume that you smell is made of such particles.

But how do you think the mind knows any thing about these particles when they come into the nose? It is in this way. In the lining of the nose are the fine ends of the nerve of smell. These ends of the branches of this nerve are so small that you can not see them. Now the fine particles that I have told you about touch these ends of the nerve, and the nerve tells the mind about them; and this is smelling.

The nose is a more extensive organ than most people think it is. There are divisions in it. These fold on each other in such a way that there is a great deal of surface in the nose, and the ends of the nerve of smell are all on this surface.

Some animals have a very sharp smell. In them the divisions in the nose are very great in extent, and so the nerve spreads over a large surface. The dog, you know, is able to track his master by scenting his footsteps. The cat, too, has a very quick smell for rats and mice.

Some persons have a sharp smell for some things. I have heard of a blind gentleman who could always tell when there was a cat any where near him by his sense of smell. Once he was very sure that there was one near by, though no one could see her; he insisted upon it that he was right, and after a while pussy was found in a closet of the room. There was also a blind and deaf person who could distinguish between different people that he knew by the sense of smell.

The sense of smell affords us great enjoyment. The Creator has, for the purpose of gratifying us, scattered sweet-smelling flowers all over the earth. These are all perfume factories, as I told you in Part First, made by him to give us pleasure. He could have made the flowers and fruits in such a way that they would have no smell; but, in his desire to please us and make us happy, he has given to them a great variety of pleasant odors. There are, it is true, some unpleasant smells in the world, but these are not any thing like as common as the pleasant ones; and many of them are manifestly very useful in warning us of danger. For example, the unpleasant odor caused by filth and decay tells, people where these causes of disease are, so that they may get rid of them. And plants that are poisonous generally have a disagreeable odor, which leads us to avoid them.

The sense of taste is another source of gratification to us. The nerve of this sense has its fine ends mostly in the tongue. What we take into the mouth touches these ends of the nerve, and the nerve tells the mind about it; and this is tasting.

Besides the pleasure which we have from the taste,

the great use of this sense is to guide us in the choice of food. Animals choose the kinds of food that are proper for them, and they do it by their taste. They very seldom make a mistake in this. The sense of taste, like that of smell, sometimes warns us of danger. If out food tastes bad, we know that there is something wrong about it and do not eat it, and so, perhaps, avoid being made sick.

The sense of touch gives a great deal of knowledge to the mind. This sense has a large number of nerves in all parts of the body, and they are making reports continually to the mind. Especially busy in this way are the nerves of the tips of the fingers. It is by the fine ends of these nerves that the mind finds out how different things feel. It finds out whether they are soft or hard, smooth or rough, etc.

These nerves in the tips of the fingers are of great service to the mind in guiding it in using the muscles. In playing with the fingers on an instrument, the feeling in the ends of them is a guide to the mind in working them. So it is with any thing that we do with them. You could not do some of the simplest things if there was no feeling in your fingers. You could not even button and unbutton your coat. I shall have more to say about this when I tell you particularly about the hand.

The nerves of touch are not placed on the surface of the skin. We have really two skins, an outer and an inner one. The nerves are in the inner skin, and are covered by the outer skin. This outer skin is very thin except on the sole of the foot and the palm of the hand; from its thin-ness it is called the scarf-skin. It is this which is raised when a blister is drawn; and perhaps you know that it does not hurt to prick this when we want to let the water out; but if the needle touches the inner skin, where the nerves are, you feel it very quickly.

Now, when you touch any thing, the nerves in the inner skin feel it through this scarf-skin. This is so thin and soft that the nerves can feel through it; and, at the same time, it is a good protection to them. If it were not for this, the nerves would be affected too much by the rubbing of things against them. They could not even bear the air. If you had no scarf-skin you would be in great distress all the time. You know how much pain you suffer if you rub off the skin, as it is called, any where. It is the scarf-skin only that is rubbed off, and this exposes to the air the fine ends of the nerves in the inner skin.

The ends of the nerves of touch are in rows on the tips of the fingers. It is these rows that make the curved lines that you can see so plainly.

There are no animals that have such perfect instruments of touch as our fingers are. Animals that have hoofs, as the horse and the cow, can not feel much with their fore feet. They have their sense of touch mostly in their lips and tongues. The elephant has this sense chiefly in the finger-shaped thing at the end of his trunk. There is not much feeling in the paws of dogs, cats, etc. The whiskers of the cat are feelers. There are nerves at the root of each of those long hairs, so that when any thing touches the whiskers the cat's mind knows it at once.

Insects have feelers extending out from their heads.

Sometimes they are very long, as you see in this insect, called the ichneumon fly. We see insects, as they are going about, touch things with these feelers as we do with our hands. Bees can work in the dark, in their hives, guided by their feelers; indeed, the bee will not work at all if his feelers are cut off: he does not seem to know what to do with himself. Insects sometimes appear to tell each other things by their feelers. In every hive of bees there is a queen. If she dies, those that know about it go around very quickly, telling the other bees by striking their feelers with their own; and those that are told tell others, and thus the sad event is soon known all over the hive.

*Questions.*— By which senses does the mind get most of its knowledge? What is fragrance? How does the mind know any thing about it? What is said of the extent of the organ of smell? What is said of the smell of some animals? Of the acute smell of some persons? What is said of the enjoyment afforded by the sense of smell? How are offensive odors sometimes useful? What is said of the sense of taste? What are its uses? Where is the sense of touch? Where is it especially active? What do the nerves of touch in the fingers tell the mind? In what way do they help us in using the muscles? Tell about the two skins of our bodies. Why is the outer skin needed? What makes the curved lines on the tips of the fingers? What is said of touch in animals that have hoofs? What are the whiskers of the cat for? What is said of the feelers of insects? What is told about the bees?

## CHAPTER XV

## THE BONES.

I HAVE told you, in the last few chapters, how it is that the mind learns about the world around it by the senses. But the mind does something besides learn. It tells others about what it learns. It does this by the muscles in various ways. When you tell any thing by speaking, it is the muscles of the throat, and mouth, and chest that do it. When you write, the muscles of your hand are telling what the mind directs them to tell. When your face expresses your thoughts and feelings, it is the muscles of the face that tell what the mind thinks and feels.

The mind not only tells things, but it does things also, and it does them by the muscles. You see a man busily at work making something: his muscles are doing the work. The mind is directing them how to do it by the nerves that spread to them from the brain. How does his mind know in what way to direct them? It is by knowledge gained through the senses—by his eyes and ears. He has seen people do the same kind of work and they have told him about it. His mind uses with the muscles what it has learned by the senses.

You see, then, that the mind makes use of what it learns by the senses in two ways: it tells about it, and it uses it in doing things; and in both telling and doing it uses the muscles. Our knowledge, then, goes into the mind by the senses—they are its *inlets*; but it comes out by the muscles—they are its *outlets*. If a mind were in a body that had the senses, but had no muscles, it might know a great deal, but it could never let any body know what it knew, and it could not do any thing.

The chief things that are moved in the body by the muscles are the bones, and I shall tell you about these before I tell you about the muscles.

When you bend your arm, the muscles make the bones in the lower part of the arm bend on the bone in the upper part. There is a joint at the elbow for this purpose; and there are joints in many other parts of the body, so that the muscles can move one bone upon another.

These joints of the bones are so contrived that they do not wear out. They work nicely through a long life. Now it would be very strange if a joint in a machine should work all the time for seventy or eighty years, and still be almost as good as new. No man ever made such a joint.

You know that men keep oiling the joints in machinery. If they did not, the joints would soon wear out. When the cars stop at a station, you see men with tin vessels oiling the boxes of the wheels of the locomotive and the cars, and other parts that rub on each other. The joints of our bones need no such care from us. We never need to oil them as men oil machinery. They are very nicely made. The ends of the bones are tipped with a very smooth substance, and this is always kept in good order; and then, too, the joints always keep themselves oiled. How this is done I explain in a book for older scholars.

The bones are the frame-work of the body. They are to the body what whalebones are to an umbrella, what timbers are to a house, or what the ribs of leaves are, as I told you in Part First, to the leaves. The bones make the body firm. You could not stand up if you had no bones; you would have to crawl like the worm. See one bracing himself to pull or push. The bones are all pressed tightly against each other by the strong muscles.

The bones of the body have very different shapes and

sizes. Let us look at some of them.

The bones of the head, represented here, make a roundish box. This is to hold the brain. Here the mind, the governor of all the machinery of the body, resides. Great care is therefore taken to guard well this upper room of the body. Its bony walls are made very strong.

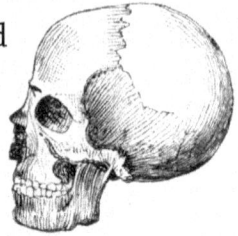

Look at this barrel-shaped set of bones that make the chest. The ribs go round it as hoops do round a barrel. They are joined to the back bone behind and to the breast bone in front. They are joined to the back bone in such a way that they move up and down as you breathe. You can feel them move upward if you put your hand on your chest as you take a full breath. Inside of this barrel-shaped set of bones are the heart and lungs.

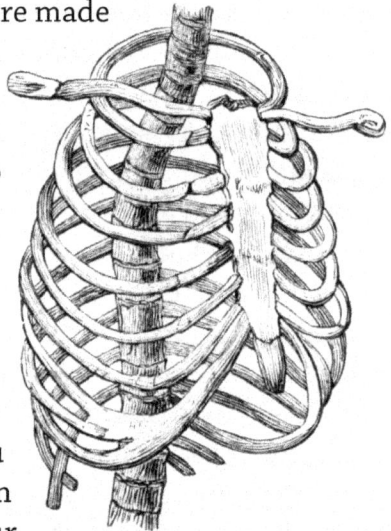

The back bone, as we call it, is not one bone; it is a chain or pile of twenty-four bones placed one above another. You can see a part of this pile or column, as it is sometimes called, in the figure of the bones of the chest. If it were all one bone, you could not twist your body about as you do. And in making a bow, you could not bend your back. You could only bend your head forward on the top of the back bone, and bend your body forward on your lower limbs. A very awkward bow that would be. As it is, whenever you make a bow, there is a little motion between each two of the whole twenty-four bones, and this makes the bow easy and graceful. Persons that bow stiffly do not have enough of this movement in the column of bones, but move it altogether, very much as if it were all one bone.

The head rests on the top of this column of bones. When you move your head backward and forward, it rocks on the topmost bone of this column. There are two little smooth places hollowed out on this bone for it to rock on, and the head has two smooth rockers that fit into these places.

*Questions.*— In what two ways does the mind use what it learns? With what does it do this? What are the inlets of the mind's knowledge? What are its outlets? What move the bones on each other? What is said about the wearing of the joints? What is said about their being kept oiled? What are the bones to the body? What is said about the bones of the head? What of the bones of the chest? To what are the ribs fastened behind? To what in front? How many bones are there in what is called the back bone? Why are there so many? What does the head rest on? What is said about the motion of the head?

## CHAPTER XVI

## MORE ABOUT THE BONES.

HERE ARE the bones of the arm and the hand. The head of the arm bone that goes into the socket at the shoulder is, as you see, a smooth round ball. It fits into a sort of cup. The joint here is what we call a ball-and-socket joint. The ball turns in the socket very easily in making any whirling motion with your arm, as you do when you jump the rope.

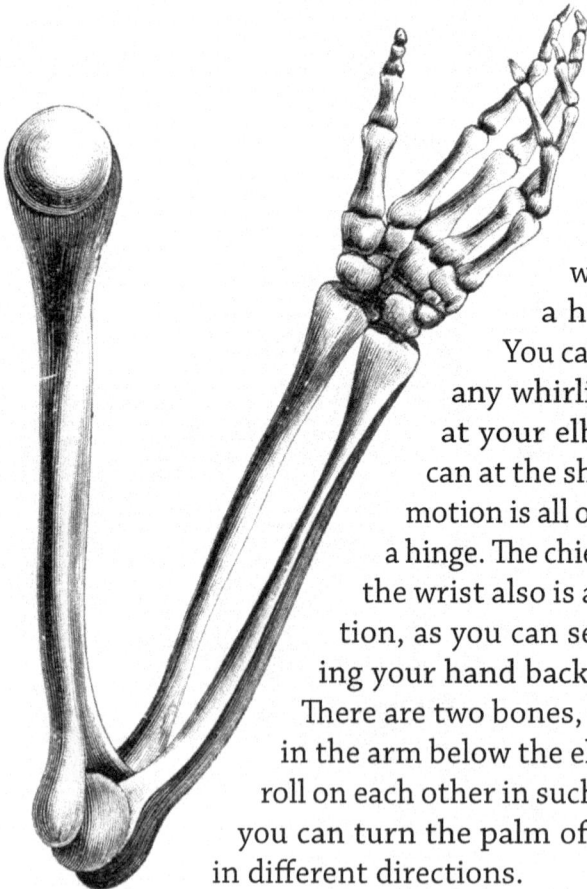

The joint at the elbow is of a different kind: it is what we call a hinge joint. You can not make any whirling motion at your elbow as you can at the shoulder; the motion is all one way, like a hinge. The chief motion at the wrist also is a hinge motion, as you can see by working your hand back and forth. There are two bones, you notice, in the arm below the elbow: these roll on each other in such a way that you can turn the palm of your hand in different directions.

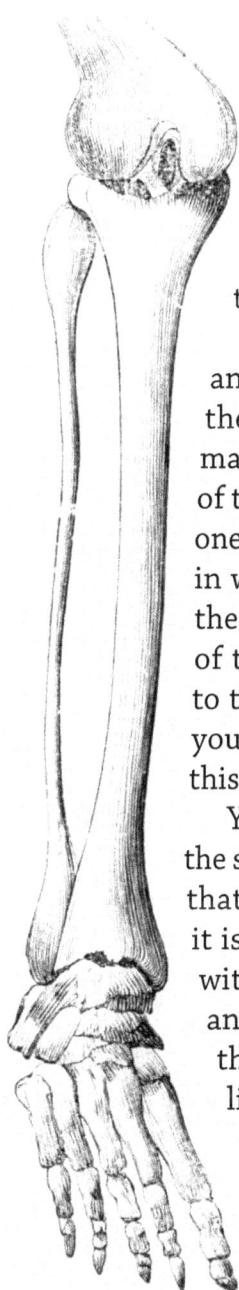

There are a great many little bones in the body of the hand and in the fingers. There is a very great variety in their motions, so that the hand can do almost any thing that you want it to do. I shall have something more to tell you about this when you come to the chapter on the hand.

You have here the bones of the leg and foot. You see only the lower end of the stout thigh bone, at the knee joint: it makes a hinge joint with the large bone of the leg. The motion of this joint is only one way, backward and forward, as you see in walking. The small, thick bone, called the knee-pan, is left out in the figure. One of the uses of this bone is to be a shield to the joint. If you fall down in running, you are apt to come upon the knee, and this shield keeps the joint from being hurt.

You see that long, very slender bone at the side of the large one: one would suppose that this would be very easily broken, but it is not, because it is so well covered up with muscles. Its lower end is quite thick and strong, and makes the outer part of the ankle. The ankle joint is a hinge joint like that of the knee.

There are as many bones in the foot as there are in the hand. Why is this? You remember that I told you that the hand had so many bones because it had to perform so many different motions. But it is not so with the foot; it does not have much variety of motion. There is some other reason, then, for its having so many bones. It is this. If the bones of the foot were all in one, the foot would be a very stiff and clumsy thing; it would not be springy as it is now. You would make awkward work in walking and running with such feet.

The bones of different animals are made differently, according to the work which they do. Those that do heavy work have heavy, stout skeletons; but those that have only light work to do have their bones slender. A bird has a light skeleton, for it could not fly so well with a heavy one. Here is the skeleton of a bat. The bones are exceedingly light and slender, for it is light and nimble work that he does in flying.

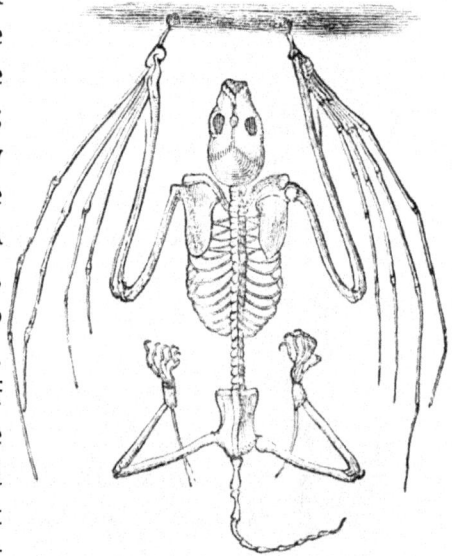

The bones in an old person are more brittle than those in a child. If the child's bones were brittle they would be very often broken, because he so often tumbles down. If old persons were as careless as children are, there would be broken limbs to be taken care of in almost every house. They would not get off with a short crying spell and a bruise, as children commonly do when they have a fall.

There is one contrivance in the child's head that prevents the bones from breaking in its frequent falls. In the grown person the bones of the head are fastened tightly together, and are almost like one bone. But it is not so with the child. In an infant's head they are very loose, and you can feel quite a space between the bones at the top of his forehead. Now, when the child falls and hits his head, the loose bones give and do not break.

Though the teeth are like the bones, they are different from them in one thing. The bones grow with the rest of the body, but the teeth never grow any larger than they are at first. When the tooth first pushes up through the gum, it is as large as it ever will be. Look at the reason of this. The outside of the tooth—the enamel, as it is called—is made very hard. It needs to be so, that the tooth may do its work well. Such a hard substance, when once made, is finished. It never can grow. No blood can get into it to make it grow, as it can into the bones.

And now you see the reason that every person has two sets of teeth. If the teeth that one has when a child should remain in his head, they would be too small for him when he became an adult; and as the jaws grew they would become quite far apart, and so would look very strange. To get rid of these difficulties, the first set begin to be shed about the seventh year, and a new set of larger teeth take their places. As the new teeth are not only larger, but are more in number, they fill up all the room designed for them in the enlarged jaws.

All the bones of our bodies are inside, and are covered with muscles, cords, and ligaments; and over all is the skin. But the bones of some animals are outside. This is the case with crabs and lobsters. Their bones make a sort of coat of mail to defend the soft parts from being injured. The hard coats of many insects also may be considered as their skeletons.

Such animals as crabs and lobsters have new skeletons every year. The old skeletons are too small for their growing bodies, and so they must be cast off. The animal crawls into a retired place to go through the operation. It is painful, and sometimes proves even fatal. He makes a great effort, and the shell comes apart. He then, by hard struggling, pulls himself out. He now keeps still a few days in his retirement, and another case or skeleton, as hard as the old one, is formed. When he comes out with his new armor on, he is as brave and as ready to fight as ever.

*Questions.*— What is said about the shoulder joint? The elbow joint? The wrist? How is it that you can turn the palm of the hand one way and another? Why are there so many little bones in the hand? What is said about the knee joint? What is one of the uses of the knee-pan? What is said about the slender bone in the leg? What about the ankle joint? Why are there so many bones in the foot? What is said of the difference in brittleness between the bones of the old and of the young? What is said about the bones in a child's head? How are the teeth unlike the bones? Why do we have two sets of teeth? What is said about the bones of some animals? What is related of crabs and lobsters?

## CHAPTER XVII

## THE MUSCLES.

I HAVE already told you some things about the muscles. There is no motion in the body that is not made by them. They move the bones, and they move other parts also, as the tongue, the corners of the mouth, the eyes, the eyelids, etc.

But you will want to know how they do this. Stretch a strip of India-rubber with your hands. Now let it go, and it will shorten itself. When a muscle pulls a bone, it shortens itself just as this strip of India-rubber does. But the cause of its shortening itself is different. The mind makes the muscle shorten. You think to bend your arm; and, as quick as thought, something goes by nerves to the muscle that can do this, and it shortens itself and bends the arm.

Here is a figure that shows the muscle that bends the arm, and also the muscle that straightens it out. All the other muscles of the arm are left out, so that you may see just how these operate. Look at the muscle marked *a*: you can see that when this shortens itself it must pull up the forearm, that is, that part of the arm which is below the elbow. The muscle *b* has a contrary effect. The end of this muscle is fastened to the point of the elbow, and when it shortens it pulls the forearm down and straightens the arm.

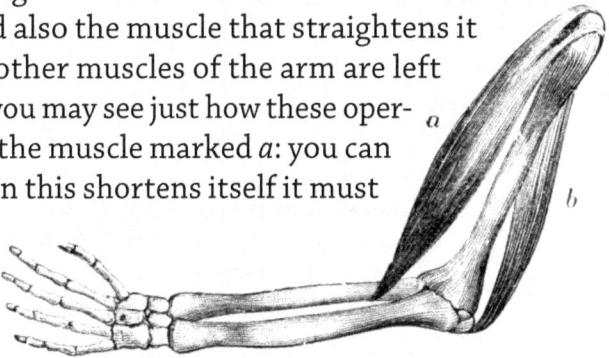

When a muscle shortens itself, it swells out and be-comes hard. Straighten your arm, and then take hold of it with your other hand a little above the elbow; now bend up your arm as forcibly as you can, and you will feel the muscle on the front of the arm swell out and harden as you hold your hand upon it.

The muscles are the fleshy part of the body. The meat of animals is made up of muscles. They are not of the same color in all animals. In some they are quite red, while in others they are of a light color. Beef—the meat of the ox or the cow—is, you know, a deep red, and is very dif-ferent from the meat of a fowl. The muscles of fishes are generally very light in color.

Your arm below the elbow is very fleshy. Most of the muscles that move the fingers, as well as those that move the hand, are there. Take hold of that part of the arm with your other hand while you work the fingers back and forth, and you will feel the muscles as they shorten themselves to pull the fingers. Here is a figure show-ing the muscles in this fleshy part of the arm. You see

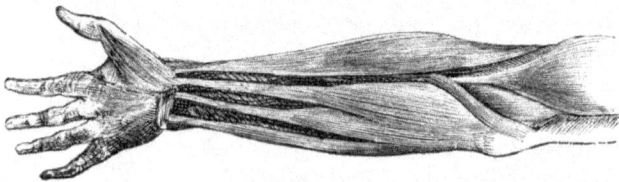

that they are quite large. The wrist is very slender. There are no muscles there; there are bright, shining, smooth cords there, that run from the muscles to the fingers. The muscles pull the fingers by these cords just as men pull any thing by ropes. You can see the play of these cords very plainly on the back of the hand of a thin person as the fingers are worked.

There are only some very small muscles in the hand, as those that spread the fingers out, and those that bring them together again. If you work your fingers in this way, you will see that the muscles, which do such light work, need not be large and strong. The muscles that do the hard work of the hand are up in the arm. They are very large. If they were not, you could not grasp things so tightly, and pull so hard as you sometimes do.

Now see why it is that these large muscles are put so far away from where they do their work. If they were put in the hand, they would make it a large and clumsy thing. They are therefore put up in the arm, where there is room for them, and they have small, but very strong cords by which they pull the fingers. They give to the arm that round fullness that makes its shape so beautiful.

You can see the same kind of arrangement in the drum-stick, as it is called, of the fowl. The large muscles that work the claws are up in the full, round part of the leg, and there are small, stout cords that extend from them down to the claws. Children often amuse themselves with pulling these cords in the drum-stick of a fowl, making the claws move just as they are moved by the muscles of the animal when he is alive.

It is with the muscles that move the toes as it is with those that move the fingers. They are put mostly up in the leg, and their slender tendons, by which they pull, go down over the ankle to the toes, just as in the arm the tendons go over the wrist to the fingers. If the muscles of the toes were all put in the foot, they would make it very clumsy, and at the same time the leg would be ugly from the want of that fullness which it now has.

Both at the wrist and the ankle the tendons are bound down very tightly. If this were not so they would be always flying out of place, stretching out the skin before them in ridges. This would be the case especially with the tendons that go to the toes. Every time that the muscles pulled on them, they would start out very much at the bend of the ankle if they were not firmly held by the ligaments.

The muscles are of many shapes—round, flat, long, short, etc. They are shaped to suit the work which they are to do.

They vary much in size also. Some are very large, and some are exceedingly small. How large are the muscles of the arm that wield the hammer and the axe! But how small are the muscles that work the musical cords in your throat when you speak or sing! These little muscles make all the different notes of the voice by pulling on these cords, and in doing this many of their motions are exceedingly slight.

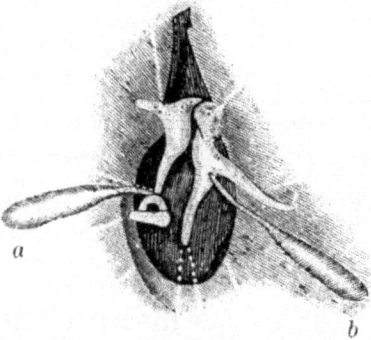

You remember that in the chapter on the hearing I told you about the little bones in the ear. These have some very little muscles which move them. The bones and the muscles, a and b, are represented in the following figure. The muscles, you see, have tendons or cords to pull by, in the same way that the muscles in the arm have. Both the bones and the muscles are larger in this figure than they are in the body. As the bones are the smallest ones that we have, so it is with the muscles. Very small machinery is this part of the hearing machinery.

The birds that go swiftly on their wings have very large muscles to work them. This gives them the full, round breast which you see that they have. But the muscles that work the musical cords in their little throats, as they sing so sweetly, are so small that it is difficult to find them.

*Questions.*— By what is all motion in the body made? What do the muscles move? Explain how the muscles move things. Tell about the two muscles of the arm in the figure. What is said about the swelling out of the muscles as they shorten? What is the meat of animals? What is said about the color of muscles in different animals? What is said of the muscles in the arm below the elbow? What is said of the wrist? What of the muscles in the hand? Why are most of the muscles that move the fingers put up in the arm? What is said about the drum-stick of a fowl? What is said about the muscles of the toes? What about the ligaments of the tendons at the wrist and ankle? What is said of the shapes of muscles? What of their sizes? What are the smallest muscles in the body? What is said about the muscles of birds used in flying and those used in singing?

## CHAPTER XVIII

## MORE ABOUT THE MUSCLES.

THERE IS a great number of muscles in the whole body to produce all its motions. There are about fifty in each arm and hand. In the whole body there are about four hundred and fifty, and each muscle is made up of a great number of fibres or threads, every fibre having its own work to do.

Now all these muscles have nerves that connect them with the brain, and the mind tells them by these nerves just what to do. Each muscle has a great many little nervous ends scattered through it every where. The message from the mind that tells the muscle to act does not go to the whole muscle as one thing, as a message is sent to a person. It goes to each fibre of it, telling that fibre what to do. Every fibre of the muscle has its little nervous tube connecting it with the brain, for the nerves are bundles of tubes, just as the muscles are bundles of fibres. And each fibre gets its messages from the mind separate from all the other fibres by its own tube, so that each fibre is a workman by itself. How well these workmen pull together when they all get a message from your mind by their telegraphic tubes!

Commonly it takes several muscles to make any motion, and sometimes many muscles act together. When this is so, messages are sent to a great multitude of fibres in these many muscles. Think of this. Raise your hand. It is not one muscle that does this, but many. Your mind has sent a message to all the fibres of these muscles, and they have all done their part in raising your hand. But now raise it again a little differently. A different message for this has been sent to all the fibres; and so for all the different motions there are different messages. It does not seem possible that so many different messages should be sent through the nerves to the fibres of all the muscles, and that these fibres should obey them so perfectly.

This is wonderful even in so simple a motion as raising the hand; but how much more wonderful when a great variety of rapid motions are made by the muscles, as in playing on a piano! How busy is the mind of the player in sending its messages, one after the other, to the multitudes of muscular fibres that work the arms and the fingers! And if he sings at the same time that he plays, his mind is sending messages also to the muscles of the chest, and throat, and mouth. And what adds greatly to the wonder is, that all this time that the mind is sending out so many messages, it is receiving messages from the senses. Messages are going from the sounds of the piano and the voice along the nerves of the ear to the mind. They go also from the tips of the busy fingers as they press the keys. How wonderful that all these messages are going back and forth so rapidly, and the mind in the brain manages them without any confusion!

I have told you that there are some parts besides bones that are moved by muscles. Different

parts of the face are moved by them, and it is this that gives it its different expressions. Thus, when you are pleased and laugh, the muscles pull up the corners of the mouth. If you laugh very hard, they pull them up very much, as you see in the face drawn here. See how this face is wrinkled under the eyes. This is because the muscles pull at the corners of the mouth so hard as to push up the cheeks.

What do you think the difference is between laughing and smiling? It is this. In laughing, the corners of the mouth are drawn up a good deal, but in smiling they are drawn up only a little. Most people think that the eyes have a great deal to do with laughing and smiling, and they talk about a laughing eye and a pleasant eye. But this is not correct. It is these muscles, which pull up the corners of the mouth, that make the eye look pleasant and laughing; indeed, laughing and smiling can be done with the eyes shut. We often see a beautiful smile in the face of the sleeping infant. It is because some pleasant dream in his mind plays on the nerves that go to his smiling muscles.

There are muscles to pull the corners of the mouth down, and these make the face look sad; and if the muscles that wrinkle the eyebrows act at the same time, the face is both sad and cross, as you see here. Observe just what the difference is between this face and the laughing face on the opposite page. The difference is merely in the corners of the mouth and in the eyebrows. In this face the two wrinklers of the eyebrows are in action, and so are the two muscles that pull down the corners of the mouth. Four small muscles, then, make this face sad and cross. But in the laughing face the eyebrow-wrinklers are quiet, and the corners of the mouth are pulled up instead of being pulled down. It is the two little muscles that pull up the corners of the mouth that do all the laughing in the face.

You have often heard the expressions, "He had a down look," and "His countenance fell." These refer to the effect produced by sadness on the corners of the mouth. This explains also the meaning of the common expression, "Down in the mouth."

There is a certain muscle called the proud muscle. It pushes up the under lip. It is chiefly by this that pouting, that ugly expression so common with some children, is done. When the eyebrow-wrinklers act at the same time, there is scowling with the pouting, and then the face is very ugly. I beseech of you not to get into the habit of using these cross muscles. Keep always pleasant and kind, and then those nice little muscles that draw up the corners of the mouth will always be ready to light up your face with a cheerfulness that shall be pleasant to look upon.

There are some animals that have certain muscles in the face that we have not. These are the snarling muscles. They pull up the lip at the sides of the mouth so as to show the long, tearing teeth. You see them in operation in the dog, the tiger, etc., when they are angry. No animal but man has in the face either the frowning, or the sad, or the smiling muscles. Perhaps you will say that the dog smiles when he is pleased and looks up at his master. He smiles, it is true, but he does it only with his wagging tail, for he has no muscles in his face to do it with.

How wonderful is the variety of expression in the human face! And yet all is caused by a few muscles, and the principal ones are those that draw up and draw down the corners of the mouth, and those that wrinkle the eyebrows.

*Questions.*— How many muscles are there in the arm and hand? How many in the whole body? What is each muscle made up of? What is said of the fibres? Is it common for a motion to be made by one muscle alone? What is said about raising the arm in different ways? What is said about the variety of rapid motions that are sometimes performed? What gives the face its different expressions? How is laughing done? What makes the wrinkling under the eyes in laughing? What is the difference between laughing and smiling? Has the eye any thing to do with them? What is said about the sad muscles? What about the cross ones? What is the difference between a cross and sad face and a laughing one? What is said about certain expressions in common use? What is said about the muscles of expression in the face of animals? What is said of the variety of expression in the human face?

CHAPTER XIX.

## THE BRAIN AND NERVES IN ANIMALS.

I HAVE told you how your mind learns about the world around you, and how it makes use of its knowledge by means of the machinery of your body—the muscles, bones, etc. Your mind is in the brain, and uses the brain to think with; and from the brain branch out all the nerves by which it works all the various machinery of the body. Your brain, then, may be considered the central workshop of your mind; or it is like an engine-room of a factory, where the engine is that keeps the machinery in other parts of the building in motion.

The different animals have a brain and nerves just as you have, and their minds in their brains learn about things around them. They do not learn so much as your mind does, it is true; but they really do learn. If you look at a kitten when it is first born, it is very much like a baby. It does not know any thing. But, like the baby, it knows more and more every day, and when it gets to be a cat it knows a great deal; and all that it knows has come to its mind in the same way as what you know has come into your mind. It has come in through its senses. All its knowledge came in at its eyes and ears, etc., and got to its brain by the nerves.

The mind in animals, too, uses the muscles in the same way that your mind does. Watch a kitten at play. The muscles that move her paws are directed by her mind in the brain by means of the nerves. As she pokes at the thing that you hold out to her, the nerves of her eyes are telling the mind in the brain all the time about the string, and then the mind is telling the muscles of the paws what to do. See her as she springs to catch the string that you draw along on the floor. As she watches it, messages are going from those bright eyes to her mind in the brain; and then, as she springs, messages are sent from her brain to a great many muscles in different parts of her body. The mind tells the muscles just when and how to act, and they all do exactly as the mind tells them. The mind of a cat sets a great deal of machinery at work when she makes a spring to catch any thing.

What I have told you about some animals is true of all. The little insect that flies out of the way when you strike at him has a little brain, and there his mind thinks about what it sees, and hears, and feels, etc., just as your mind does; and when he flies away so quickly from the blow that his eyes see coming, his mind tells the muscles to make the wings go. There are nerves that carry messages from his senses to the mind in his brain, and there are nerves that carry messages from his brain to his muscles, as there are in you. The brain is very small, and the nerves are very fine, but they do their work well. They make a little telegraph, but it is a good one.

What a quantity of thinking there is done in the brains of all the animals in the world! How busy their minds are, receiving reports from their senses, and working all the machinery of their bodies. Go out into the garden, and see the birds, the butterflies, the bees, the flies, the ants, the frogs, the toads, and the worms; they are all busy thinking. They can not move without thinking. It is their thinking that makes their muscles move them. And they think about what they move for.

Some of them think more than others. The bird thinks more than the worm. Some think faster than others.

The humming-bird, that darts so quickly from flower to flower, thinks as fast as he works. But the lazy toad is a slow thinker. His mind does not work the machinery of his muscles much, and so does but little thinking. But even he once in a while thinks quickly. Let a fly walk along pretty near him, and he will catch it with his tongue so quickly that you can not see just how he does it. He watches the fly intently, keeping very still all the while; and when it gets near enough, he thrusts out his tongue, and the fly is gone. You would hardly think that so lazy-looking an animal could do any thing so quickly. But he is nimble as a fly-catcher, if he is not nimble at any thing else; and very quickly must the mind in his brain think when it is working its fly-catching machinery.

The more an animal thinks, the larger is the brain as compared with the rest of the body. Man thinks more than any other animal, and so he has a large brain. But the oyster has hardly any thing that can be called a brain, for in his still life, shut up as he is in his shell, he thinks but little. But such animals as horses, dogs, cats, birds, monkeys, etc., have quite large brains, for they think a great deal. Their brains, however, are not, by any means, as large as the brain of man is in proportion to the size of the body.

This is as we should suppose it would be. The brain is the machinery with which the mind thinks. Now, whenever we see a great deal of machinery together at work, we know that it is because there is much to be done by it; and when we see a small machine that has not many different parts, we know that it is not intended to do much. So it is with the mind's thinking machinery. The brain of an animal that thinks but little is small and simple; but the brain of one that thinks much is large and has many parts. Though animals do their thinking with their brains as we do with ours, there is some thinking that we do that they can not. There are some things about which they know nothing. But I will tell you about this in another chapter.

*Questions.*— What does your mind do with your brain? How is your brain like the engine-room of a factory? What is said about the minds of different animals? How is a kitten, when it is first born, like a baby? How does it learn? What is said about the mind, and brain, and nerves of an insect? What is said about the quantity of thinking done in the brains of animals? How do some differ from others in their thinking? Tell about the toad. What is said about the size of the brain in different animals? How is the brain compared with machinery?

## CHAPTER XX

## THE VARIETY OF MACHINERY IN ANIMALS.

YOU HAVE seen what a variety of curious machinery there is in our bodies for our minds to work, besides that which is needed to keep the body in repair. But I have told you some things about other animals as I have gone along. There is in them also a great deal of machinery, and it is different in each. The variety of it is wonderful. You see that the world is every where full of many kinds of animals, making it a very busy world. I do not believe that you have ever thought how different they are from each other. I will therefore tell you a little about this.

See what a difference there is between man and some animals. Look at the oyster. He lives in the water, shut up in his rough shell. He is no traveler. He has no eyes to see sights with. He has no sense of smell. He has taste for his food, and, no doubt, enjoys it. He has the sense of touch; this he needs, both to manage his food and to guard himself against harm. As he does not move about, and has no feet or hands, he has but few muscles. He has one to shut up his shell tight, which he does when he is alarmed. His brain and nerves are very small affairs, for he has little use for such things.

There is little machinery, then, in an oyster, as you compare it with the machinery in your body; and it is simply because he does not need so much as you do. If he had needed more, God would have given it to him. But there is, after all, considerable machinery even in the oyster. He has machinery for digesting his food. He has circulating machinery—a heart with its arteries and veins. And he has gills like fishes, by which his blood is aired by the air in the water. Then he has a few muscles, some nerves, and a sort of brain.

Look, now, at another animal that has less contrivances in him than the oyster. Look at the hydra. This is a very little animal which is found in ponds, sticking to a straw or stick by a sort of sucker. Here is a representation of it. The small figure shows it of its natural size. The larger figure shows it as magnified by the microscope. This animal is little else than a stomach with long arms. We can turn the body of it—that is, the stomach, inside out, and the animal will do as well as before. The arms are merely to catch things, as worms and insects, which they put into the mouth of the stomach, marked *a*. One of the arms is represented as having caught something, which it is about to put into this mouth. When the little creature is alarmed, he gathers up all his arms around his stomach, and looks like a little ball. No brain has ever been discovered in him, but it is plain that he thinks some in catching his food, and in gathering himself into a ball to escape notice. He probably has a brain to think with, though it is so small that it is not to be seen with the most powerful microscope.

On the following page is one of the arms of this animal as seen with a powerful microscope. It is made up of little cells or bladder-like things. How it is that these make the different motions of this arm we do not know.

The two animals that I have just told you about are very unlike to man, but they are not more so than a multitude of others. The variety in the shapes of animals and in the arrangements of their different parts is almost endless; but, with all this variety, all are alike in some things. All have organs to digest their food with, and organs to circulate their blood. All have brains to think with, and nerves to use in finding out about what is around them, and in making their muscles work.

The variety in the contrivances in animals is so great, that when one undertakes to study them, he continually finds something new. And one thing is always true of the machinery in animals—it is perfect. It is always exactly fitted to do just what it is made for. No machinery that man ever made is equal to it.

Animals are suited in their shapes and arrangements to the way in which they live. Some are made to fly. These have wings; and the wings exhibit great variety, as you see if you look at the birds and insects that are so busy in the air. Some animals are made to live in the water; most of these have a broad tail and fins to swim with, but some crawl, as the crab. Some float about, like the hydra, and some lie still, like the oyster.

Some animals walk about on the ground. Man is the only animal that walks about erect upon two feet. The beasts, you know, are four-footed. The monkey is one of the most singular of beasts: he has neither feet nor hands, but some things which are like both. With these he is more of a climber than a walker. There are many small

animals that walk on many
feet. And the snakes, without any feet, crawl along
the ground. Some animals
hop, as the frog and toad.
Some go by a long jump,
as the grasshopper, and
the troublesome little flea,
which is here represented as
magnified by the microscope. Very strong muscles must
this animal have to enable it to make such leaps with its
long, crooked legs.

There is great variety in the coverings of animals. But
I will tell you about these in another chapter.

Some animals are much more like man than others.
The bones, and muscles, and nerves, and heart, and brain
of some are very much like the same things in our bodies.
This is true of many of the four-footed animals. You can
therefore know how the parts of the machinery inside of
you look by observing the different parts of animals at
the meat-market. In a calf's head you can see how your
brain looks. Its lungs, or lights, as they are commonly
called, are very much like yours, and its heart is quite
like your heart. And so of other parts.

The more an animal moves, the more muscles he has to
make his motions with. Man has more variety of motion
than any other animal, and so has more muscles. God
gives to each animal just the machinery that it needs.
Some have machinery that others do not have. Some have
very little, while others have a great deal. In our bodies
there is a great variety of machinery, for our busy minds
want to know and to do very many things.

The mind of man does more things with the hand than

with any other part of its machinery. I shall therefore now go on to tell you about the hand, and then about those things that, in different animals, answer somewhat in place of hands.

*Questions.*— What is said about the variety of machinery in the bodies of animals? What senses has the oyster? Why does he have these? What is said of his muscles? What of his brain and nerves? Why has not the oyster as much machinery in his body as there is in yours? What machinery has he? Tell all about the hydra. What is said about his brain? What are his arms made of? In what things are all animals alike? How does the machinery in animals compare with that made by man? What are the shapes and machinery of animals suited to? Tell about animals that fly—those that live in the water—those that walk. What is said about man? What is said about the monkey? Mention some animals that hop—some that make a long jump—those that crawl without feet. What animals are much like man, and in what? Why is there so great a variety of machinery in our bodies? What part of the machinery do our minds use most?

## CHAPTER XXI

## THE HAND.

MAN IS the only animal that has a hand. The monkey has something like a hand; but, if you watch him as he takes things, you will see that it is a very awkward and bungling thing compared with your hand.

The hand is often said to be a wonderful *instrument*. I would rather say that it is a wonderful *set of machinery*. An instrument or tool is commonly fitted to do only one thing, as a chisel, a spade, a saw, etc. But how many and how different things can be done with the hand!

Let us look at some things that the hand can do. See the blacksmith wielding the heavy hammer; how strongly his hand grasps the handle! See how it is done. The fingers and thumb are bent by those large muscles that are up in the arm. Now these same fingers, that grasp the hammer so strongly, and do this heavy work, can be trained to do work of the lightest and finest kind. They can take hold of the pen and write. They can move the tool of the engraver, making those fine lines that you sometimes see.

In the machines that man makes there is no such changing from coarse, heavy work to that which is fine and delicate. A machine that does heavy work does that only, and one that does fine work does that only. No man ever made a machine that would pull a large rope one moment, and the next pull a fine thread, and do the one just as well as the other. But that wonderful machine, the hand, can do this. It can grasp the rope firmly, and yet can take between its thumb and finger a thread so fine that you can hardly see it.

But the difference in the work of the hand is not merely in coarseness and fineness. It can do a great many different kinds of coarse work and a great many different kinds of fine work. The hand works very differently with different things. See how differently it manages a rope, a hammer, a spade, a hoe, a knife and fork, etc. It takes hold of them in different ways to work them. And then, as to fine work, how differently it manages a pen, an engraver's tool, a thread, a needle, etc.

If you watch people as they do different things, you can get some idea of the variety of the work that the hand can perform. See how differently the fingers are continually placed as one is playing on an instrument. You can see very well what a variety of shapes the hand can be put into if you observe a deaf and dumb person talking with his fingers. On the following page is a representation of the different ways in which the letters are made.

The most common things that we do with our hands are really wonderful. Watch one as he is buttoning up his coat: how easily his fingers do it; and yet it is a wonderful performance. Suppose a man should try to make a machine, shaped like the hand, that would do the same thing, do you think that he would succeed? It would be very strange if he did. Suppose, however, that, after working a long time, he did really succeed, and that you saw his machine, with its fingers and thumb, put a button through a button-hole in the same way that you do it with your fingers. Do you think that it could manage buttons of all sizes, large, middle-sized, and small? No; it could only button those that are of one size. The different sized buttons would require different machines; and, besides, a machine that could button up could not unbutton. But your hand is a machine that, besides but-

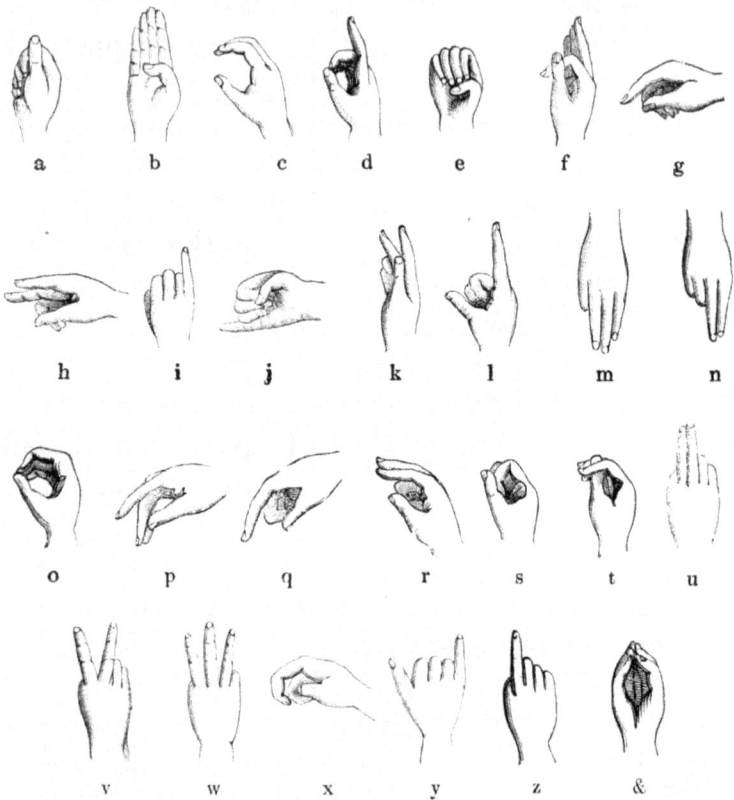

| a | b | c | d | e | f | g |

| h | i | j | k | l | m | n |

| o | p | q | r | s | t | u |

| v | w | x | y | z | & |

The *j* is made by raising the little finger as represented, and then moving it as if to make the tail of the letter. The *z* is made by raising the forefinger, and moving it in a zigzag way.

toning and unbuttoning buttons of various sizes, is doing continually a great variety of things that machines can not do. No machine can take up a pen and write, or even move a stick about as your hand can. When some ingenious man makes a machine that can do any one thing like what the hand does, it excites our wonder, and we say, How curious! how wonderful! how much like a hand it works!

But the hand is not merely a machine that performs a

great many motions; it is also an instrument with which the mind feels things. And what a delicate instrument it is for this purpose! How small are the things that you sometimes feel with the point of the finger! As you pass it over a smooth surface, the slightest roughness is felt. A great deal of knowledge, as I told you in Chapter XIV., gets into your mind through the tips of your fingers. Messages are going from them continually by the nerves to the mind in the brain. The blind, I have told you, read with their fingers. They pass them over raised letters, and the nerves of the fingers tell the mind what the letters are, just as the nerves of your eyes are now telling your mind what the letters are in this book.

Now, while the hand is performing its different motions as a machine, it is generally very much guided by this sense of touch. If your hand had no feeling in it, it would make awkward business even in such a simple operation as buttoning; and it could not do it at all if you did not look on all the time that it was doing it. Your eye-nerves would have to take the place of your finger-nerves, as in the reading of the blind the finger-nerves take the place of the eye-nerves. As it is, you need not look at your fingers while they are buttoning, for they are guided by the feeling that is in them.

There was once a woman who lost the use of one arm, and at the same time lost all her feeling in the other. She had a baby to take care of. She could hold it with the arm that had no feeling, because she could work the muscles in that arm, but she could not do it without looking at it all the time. If she looked away, the arm would stop holding the baby and let it fall, for it could not feel that it was there. In her case the eye-nerves had to keep watch in place of the arm-nerves that could not feel.

You see that the hand is different from the machines that man makes in two things—in the variety of things that it can do, and in the connection which it has with the mind by the nerves. While the mind, by the nerves, makes it do things, it knows by other nerves all the time whether it is doing them right.

See, now, what are the parts of this wonderful set of machinery. There are in the hand and arm thirty bones. There are about fifty muscles, and all these are connected with the brain by nerves. It is by them that the mind makes the muscles perform all the various motions of the hand and fingers, and then there are other nerves that tell the mind what is felt in any part of this machinery.

I have mentioned in this chapter a few of the things that are done by the hand, but there is no end to the things that can be done by this set of machinery. You can get some idea of this in two ways—by moving your hands and fingers about in all sorts of ways, and by thinking of as many as you can of the different things that people, in work or in play, do with their hands. And observe in how many more ways the hand is useful than the foot is. The foot has but a few things to do compared with the multitude of things done by the hand.

*Questions.*— What animal has something like a hand? How does it compare with your hand? Why would you call the hand a set of machinery rather than an instrument? What is said about the fingers doing heavy and light work? Tell about the rope and the thread. What is said about the different kinds of both coarse and fine work that the hand can do? What is said about playing on an instrument? What is said of the alphabet of the deaf and dumb? What is said about the common things done continually by the hand? What is said of the hand as an instrument for feeling? If your hand had no feeling, what would happen? Tell about the woman who lost the power of motion in one arm and feeling in the other. In what two things is the hand different from the machines made by man? What are the parts of the machinery of the hand? In what two ways can you get an idea of the variety of things that this machinery can do?

CHAPTER XXII.

## WHAT ANIMALS USE FOR HANDS.

THOUGH ANIMALS do not have hands, they have different parts which they use to do some of the same things that we do with our hands. I will tell you about some of these in this chapter.

You see this dog dragging along a rope which he holds in his mouth. He is making his teeth answer in place of hands. Dogs always do this when they carry things. They can not carry them in any other way. You carry a basket along in your hand, but the dog takes it between his teeth, because he has no hand as you have.

I have told you, in another chapter, how the cow and the horse crop the grass. They do it, you know, with their front teeth. They take up almost any kind of food—a potato, an apple—with these teeth. These teeth, then, answer for hands to the cow and horse. Their lips answer also the same purpose in many cases. The horse gathers his oats into his mouth with the lips. The lips are for hands to such animals in another respect. They feel things with their lips just as we do with the tips of our fingers.

My horse once, in cropping some grass, took hold of some that was so stout and so loose in the earth that he pulled it up by the roots. As he ate it the dirt troubled him. He therefore knocked the grass several times against the fence, holding it firmly in his teeth, and thus got the dirt out, just as people do out of a mat when they strike it against any thing. I once knew a horse that would lift a latch or shove a bolt with his front teeth as readily as you would with your hand. He would get out of the barnyard in this way. But this was at length prevented by a very simple contrivance. A piece of iron was fixed in such a manner at the end of the bolt that you could not shove the bolt unless you raised the iron at the same time. Probably this puzzled the horse's brain. Even if he understood it, he could not manage the two things together. I have heard about a horse that would take hold of a pump-handle with his teeth and pump water into a trough when he wanted to drink. This was in a pasture where there were several horses; and what is very curious, the other horses, when they wanted to drink, would, if they found the trough empty, tease this horse that knew how to pump; they would get around him, and bite and kick him till he would pump some water for them.

Monkeys have four things like hands. They are half way between hands and feet. With these they are very skillful at climbing. There are some kinds of monkeys, as the one represented on the following page, that use their tails in climbing as a sort of fifth hand.

The cat uses for hands sometimes her paws, with their sharp claws, sometimes her teeth, and sometimes both together. She climbs with her claws. She catches things with them—mice, rats, or any thing that you hold out for her to run after. She strikes with her paws, just as angry children and men sometimes do with their hands. When the cat moves her kittens from one place to another, she takes them up with her teeth by the nape of the neck. There is no other way in which she can do it. She can not walk on her hind feet and carry them with her fore paws. It seems as if it would hurt a kitten to carry it in the way that she does, but it does not.

When a squirrel nibbles a nut to make a hole in it, he holds it between his two fore paws like hands. So also does the dormouse, which you see here.

The bill of a bird is used as its hand. It gathers with it its food to put into its crop. When you throw corn out to the hens, how fast they pick it up, and send it down into their crops to be well soaked! The humming-bird has a very long bill, and in it lies a long, slender, and very delicate tongue. As he poises himself in the air before a flower, his wings fluttering so quickly that you can not see them, he runs his bill into the bottom of the flower where the honey is, and puts his little long tongue into it.

The bill of the duck is made in a peculiar way. You know that it gets its food under water in the mud. It can not see, therefore, what it gets. It has to work altogether by feeling, and it has nerves in its bill for this purpose. Here is a picture of its bill, showing the nerves branching out on it. You see, too, a row of pointed things all around the edge. They look like teeth, but they are not teeth. They are used by the duck in finding its food. It manages in this way: it thrusts its bill down, and as it takes it up it is full of mud. Now mixed with the mud are things which the duck lives on. The nerves tell the duck what is good, and it lets all the rest go out between the prickles. It is a sort of sifting operation, the nerves in the sieve taking good care that nothing good shall pass out.

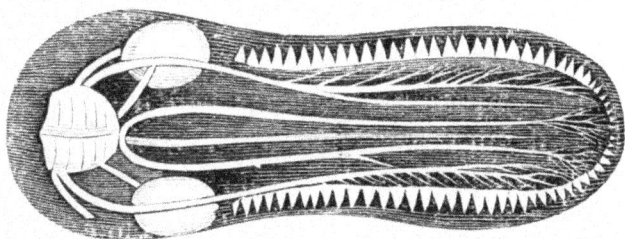

One of the most remarkable things used in place of a hand is the trunk of the elephant. The variety of uses to which the elephant puts this organ is very wonderful. It can strike very heavy blows with it. It can wrench off branches of trees, or even pull up trees by the roots, by winding its trunk around them to grasp them, as you see it is doing here. It is its arm with which it carries its young. It is amusing to see an old elephant carefully wind its trunk around a new-born elephant, and carry it gently along.

But the elephant can also do some very little things

with his trunk. You see in this picture that there is a sort of finger at the very end of the trunk. It is a very nimble finger, and with it this monstrous animal can do a great variety of little things. He will take with it little bits of bread, and other kinds of food that you hand to him, and put them into his mouth. He will take up a piece of money from the ground as easily as you can with your fingers. It is with this finger, too, that he feels of things just as you do with your fingers. I once saw an elephant take a whip with this fingered end of his trunk, and use it as handily as a teamster, very much to the amusement of the spectators.

The elephant can reach a considerable distance with his trunk. And this is necessary, because he has so very short a neck. He could not get at his food without his long trunk. Observe, too, how he can turn this trunk about in every direction, and twist it about in every way. It is really a wonderful piece of

machinery. Cuvier, a great French anatomist, says that there are over thirty thousand little muscles in it. All this army of muscles receive their orders by nerves from the mind in the brain, and how well they obey them!

You see that there are two holes in the end of the trunk. Into these he can suck water, and thus fill his trunk with it. Then he can turn the end of his trunk into his mouth and let the water run down his throat. But sometimes he uses the water in his trunk in another way; he blows it out through his trunk with great force. He does this when he wants to wash himself, directing his trunk in such a way that the water will pour over him. He sometimes blows the water out in play, for even such great animals have sports like children. Sometimes, too, he blows the water on people that he does not like. You perhaps have read the story of the tailor who pricked the trunk of an elephant with his needle. The elephant, as he was passing, put his trunk into the shop window, hoping that the tailor would give him something to eat. He was angry at being pricked, and was determined to make the man sorry for doing such an unkind act. As his keeper led him back past the same window, he poured upon the tailor his trunk full of dirty water, which he had taken from a puddle for this purpose.

*Questions.*— What is said about the dog? What answer for hands to the cow and the horse? Tell the anecdotes about horses. What does the cat use for hands, and how? What is said about the squirrel and dormouse? What is the bird's hand? Tell about feeding the hens. Tell about the bill of the duck. What is told of the humming-bird? Mention some of the variety of uses to which the elephant can put his trunk. What is said about the finger on the end of it? Why does the elephant need so long a trunk? What is said about the muscles in it? How does the elephant drink? How does he wash himself? Tell about the tailor.

## CHAPTER XXIII

## THE TOOLS OF ANIMALS.

MAN IS the only animal that makes tools to use. God has given him a mind that can contrive tools, and he has also given him hands by which he can use them. But he has given no such mind to other animals, and therefore he has not given them hands. They do not know enough to make tools, and so hands are not needed by them.

But, though other animals do not make tools, they have tools which they use. God has given them ready made, as we may say, such tools as they need. Let us look, then, at some of the tools that we find in different animals.

You see a man in the stern or hinder end of a small boat. He is sculling, as it is called. He is making the boat go by working the oar to the one side and the other. The oar is the tool or instrument by which he does it. Now a fish has an instrument like this, by which he goes through the water. His tail is like the sculling-oar that man has contrived, and which he uses with his hands. If you watch the fish as he goes through the water, you will see that he moves it to one side and the other as the man does his oar; and while he goes ahead by means of his tail, he uses his fins mostly as balancers to guide his motion. He moves them rather gently except when he wants to change his course quickly. When he is moving along fast, and wants to stop, he makes his fins stand out straight on each side. This is just as rowers in a boat use their oars when they want to stop the boat.

You see a man drilling a hole in a rock, and you hear the sound of the tool as it goes click, click, all the while. The woodpecker has a drill that works in the same way. With his bill he drills holes in the trees, and you hear the sound of his tool as you do that of the tool of the rock-blaster. It is a sort of knocking sound repeated many times very quickly.

What do you think that the woodpecker drills holes for? It is to get at worms and insects, which he eats. These are in the bark and wood of dead trunks and branches of trees. The woodpecker knows this, and so drills to find them. He does not drill into live bark and wood, for he knows that there are generally no worms or insects there.

But the woodpecker's instrument is something more than a drill. It is a drill with another instrument inside of it. This instrument is for pulling out the insect or worm that he finds in drilling. It is shown in the following figure. It is a very long, straight tongue, and ends in a bony thorn. This is, as you see, armed with sharp teeth pointing backward, like the barbs of a fish-hook. Here are, then, two instruments or tools together. And the way that the woodpecker manages them is this: while he is drilling, the two parts of the bill

are closed together, making a good wedge-pointed drill, and at the same time a snug case for the insect-catcher. As soon as he comes to an insect he opens the drill, and pushes the barbed end of his long tongue into the insect, and draws him into his mouth.

As the woodpecker has to strike so hard in drilling, the bones of his skull are made very heavy and strong. If this were not so, his drilling would jar his brain too much. And another thing is to be observed: while he is drilling he needs to stand very firmly. He must hold on tightly to the tree, or he will slip as soon as he begins to drill. He has, therefore, such claws as you see here to hold on with.

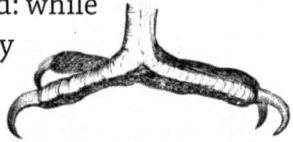

Some animals have tools to dig with. The elephant, you know, has long, strong tusks. These he uses in digging up roots of different kinds from the ground to eat. The hen digs in a small way with the claws of her feet, to find grains and other kinds of food that happen to be mingled with the earth. The pig can dig with its snout. It does not have much use for this when shut up in its pen; but let it out, and see how it will root, as we say. It does this to find things in the ground that it can eat. When the pig runs wild, it roots to get acorns and other things that become mixed up with the earth.

The mole has a similar contrivance to work in the earth with. This animal also has heavy claws with which it plows and digs. Here is a figure showing the bones of one of its fore paws. They are very heavy and strong, and are worked by large

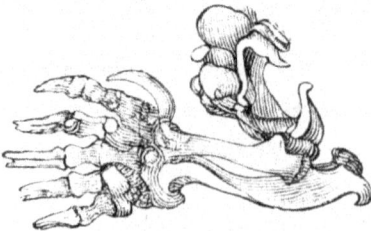

muscles. The claws on its fingers, you see, are very power-ful. The mole does great execution with this digging and plowing machine in making his tunnels and galleries in the ground.

The mole's habitation is a singular affair. It consists of a large circular room, with several galleries and passages. He makes all this in this way. He first heaps a round hill or mound, pressing the earth to make it very solid and firm; he then digs out his round room, where he lives, and the passages. You can understand how he arranges these by the figure. You can see that there are two circular galleries, one above the other, and that these are connected together by five passages. The circular room is connected with the upper gallery by three passages. It also, you see, has a deep passage out from it at the bottom, which opens into a passage that goes out from the lower gallery; this passage, and another like it on the other side, lead out into the open air. I suppose that the use of all these winding passages is to enable the mole to keep out of the way of those who want to catch it.

The marmot, or woodchuck, as he is commonly called, is a great digger. He digs his hole where he lives in this way. He loosens the dirt with his fore paws, using his teeth also when the earth is very hard, or where any roots happen to be in the way. He pushes back the dirt as he loosens it. When he gets a considerable heap, what do you think that he does with it? He shovels it out with his hinder feet, for they are so shaped that he can use them as shovels. They have a strong skin between the toes, so that when the toes are spread out the feet answer very well to shovel dirt with.

Beavers are very singular animals. They do not live alone, but many of them live together. They live in a sort of cabin, which they build with branches of trees and mud, the mud answering for mortar. In gathering the branches they often gnaw them off with their sharp and powerful teeth. They are great diggers. They dig up the earth with their paws to use in building their cabin. It is said that they use their flat tails somewhat as masons do their trowels, spatting and smoothing the coating of mud as they put it on. The tail, which you see is very stout, answers another purpose. As the beaver builds the wall of the cabin, when it gets rather high he props himself up on his tail as he works.

The beavers build their cabin close to a stream of water, and their entrance to it is below, so that they have to go down under water to get to it; and a dam is built to keep the water over this entrance of the proper height. If it were not for this, the door to the cabin might get closed up with ice if the water should get low in the stream during the winter. This dam the beavers build of branches of trees, and mud, and stones. The stones are used to make the branches stay down. In the cabin there are two rooms: in the upper one they live, and in the lower one they stow their food. This is the arrangement of these animals for the winter. In the summer they do not live together in companies, but each one makes a burrow for itself. Every autumn they come together, and unite in building their dams and cabins.

*Questions.*— Why does man make tools? Why do not other animals make them? Do they have tools? How is the swimming of a fish like sculling? What does the fish do with his fins? What is said about the bill of the woodpecker? What does he drill for? Tell about his tongue. What is said about the bones of his head? What about his claws? What is said about the digging of the elephant—of the hen—of the pig? How does the mole dig? What is said about his fore paws? Describe the arrangement of the mole's habitation. How does the woodchuck dig? How does he shovel away the dirt that he digs? Tell about the beavers. In what two ways do they use their tails? What is the arrangement of the cabin? What is the dam for?

## CHAPTER XXIV

## MORE ABOUT THE TOOLS OF ANIMALS.

INSECTS HAVE various tools or instruments. There is a fly called the saw-fly, because it really has a saw. It is a very nice one, much nicer than any saw that man ever made. The fly uses the saw to make a place to put its eggs, where they will be secure. And what is very curious, it has a sort of glue with which it fastens the eggs in their place.

There are some insects that have cutting instruments, which will cut as well as you can with scissors, if not better. There is a bee that is remarkable in this respect. It has also a boring tool. Its nest is commonly in old, half-decayed wood. It clears out a space in it with its boring instrument; it then sets itself to work with its cutting instrument to cut out pieces of leaves to line the nest and make the cells in it. These are cut of different shapes, as they are needed, as you may see in the next engraving. Below the leaves you see the nest represented. It is opened by taking off some of the wood, and there you see the lining of leaves. Great pains is taken by the bees in getting each piece of leaf of the right shape to fit well, and the

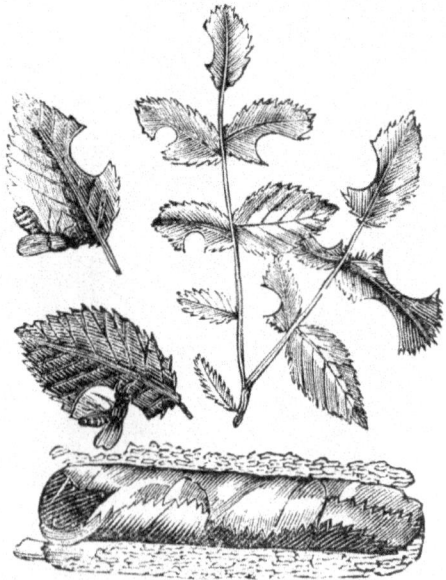

pieces are very nicely fastened together.[2]

There are some animals that have machinery for making things. All the silk that is used in the world is made by worms. The silk-worm has a regular set of machinery for spinning silk. It winds it up as it spins it. Then man unwinds it, and makes a great variety of beautiful fabrics with this silk thread.

The spinning machinery of the spider is much finer than that of the silk-worm. The thread which he spins is made up of a multitude of threads, each one of these coming out from an exceedingly small hole in the spider's body. You know that there is a large number of fibres or threads in a rope. So it is with the spider's rope, for his thread that you see, small as it is, is a rope to him. It is a rope that he walks on like a rope-dancer; and you may sometimes see him swinging upon it. Sometimes, too, he lets himself down from some height, spinning the rope that holds him as he goes down. When he does this, his spinning machine must work very briskly.

The wasp has a paper factory in him. He makes his paper out of fibres of wood, which he picks off, I suppose, with his teeth, and gathers them into a bundle. He makes this into a soft pulp in some way; then, from this, he makes the paper with which he builds his nest. It is very much, you know, like the common brown paper that man makes. The wasps work in companies, and though each one can make but little paper, they all together make their nest in a very little time. The pulp from which they make their paper is very much like the pulp from which man makes paper, and which you may see any time in the large tubs or vats of a paper factory. This pulp is generally made

---

2    A more full account of the operations of this little animal you can find in a book published by Harper and brothers, entitled Natural History, by Uncle Philip, which I recommend to my young readers as a very interesting book about animals.

from rags ground up fine, but lately wood has been much used. Perhaps the hint was taken from the wasps, who were the earliest paper-makers in the world.

Animals can not use knives and forks, as we do, in dividing up their food. They therefore have instruments given them which do this very well. Those long, sharp teeth that dogs, cats, tigers, etc., have, answer to tear to pieces the flesh they eat, as thoroughly as we can cut it up. We do not need such teeth, because with instruments contrived by man's mind for his hands to use we cut up the food sufficiently.

I have told you that the elephant can draw up water into his trunk. His trunk is therefore like the tube with which we suck up water or any liquid. And it is like a pump too, for, as I shall show you in Part Third, water is raised in the pump just as it is in a tube when we suck through it. It is with a pump something like the elephant's that many insects get the honey from the flowers. This pump is called a proboscis. It is with such an instrument that the mosquito sucks up your blood. At the end of his pump he has something with which he pierces a hole in your skin, and then he pumps your blood up into his stomach. In some insects the proboscis is very long, as you see here. This is hollow, and with it the insect sucks up the honey

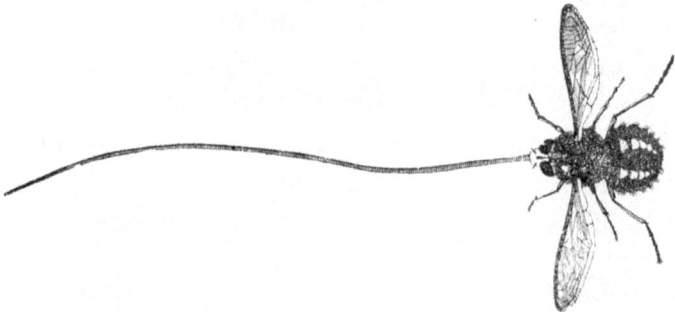

from very deep flowers, without being obliged to go to the bottom of them.

The proboscis is commonly coiled up when it is not in use. Here is the proboscis of a butterfly coiled up. The two long things above it are feelers.

The tongue of the humming-bird is really a proboscis, and a very curious one it is too. It has two tubes alongside of each other, like the two barrels of a double-barreled gun. At the tip of the tongue these tubes are a little separated, and their ends are shaped like spoons. The honey is spooned up, as we may say, and then it is drawn into the mouth through the long tubes of the tongue. But the bird uses its tongue in another way. It catches insects with it, for it lives on these as well as on honey. It does it in this way: the two spoons grasp the insect like a pair of tongs, and the tongue, bending, puts it into the bird's mouth. The tongue, then, of the humming-bird is not merely one instrument, but it contains several instruments together—two pumps, two spoons, and a pair of tongs.

The tongue of a cat is a singular instrument. It is her curry-comb. For this purpose it is rough, as you will find if you feel it. When she cleans herself so industriously, she gets off the dirt and smooths her coat just as the hostler cleans and smooths the horse's coat with the curry-comb. Her head she can not reach with her tongue, and so she has to make her fore paws answer the purpose instead.

There are some birds that live on fishes. They have instruments, therefore, purposely for catching them. The heron is a bird of this kind. He manages in this way: when the light is dim, either at dawn or when there is moonlight, it is his time for going a fishing. He will stand, as you see him here, in shallow water, so stiff and so still that he might be mistaken for a stump of a tree or something else. He is looking steadily and patiently down into the water, and the moment a fish comes along, down goes his sharp bill, and off he flies to his nest with his prey. The plumes of this singular bird are beautiful, and are very highly prized as ornaments.

There is one bird that lives chiefly on oysters. It has a bill, therefore, with which it can open an oyster-shell as skillfully as an oysterman can with his knife.

Some birds can sew very well with their beaks and feet. There is one bird that sews so well that it is called the tailor bird. Here is its nest hid in leaves which it has sewed together. It does this with thread which it makes itself. It gets cotton from the cotton-plant, and with its long, delicate bill and little feet, spins it into a thread. It then pierces the holes through the leaves with its bill, and, passing the thread through the holes, sews them together. I believe that in getting the thread through the holes it uses both its bill and its feet.

Here is a very strange-looking bird. It has no wings. It has a very long bill, which it uses in gathering its food, which consists of snails, insects, and worms. He uses his bill in another way. He often, in resting, places the tip of his bill on the ground, and thus makes the same use of his bill that an old man does of his cane when he stands leaning upon it.

There is a fish that has a singular instrument. It is a squirt-gun for shooting insects. It can shoot them not only when they are still, but when they are flying. It watches them as they are flying over the water, and hits one of them, whenever it can get a chance, with a fine stream of water from its little gun. The insect, stunned with the blow, falls into the water, and the fish eats it.

I could give you a great many more examples of the different tools that we find in animals, but these are sufficient. You can observe other examples yourselves as you look at different animals.

*Questions.*— What is said about the saw-fly? Tell about the boring and cutting instruments of a certain kind of bee. What is said about silk-worms? What about spiders? What about wasps? Why do some animals have such long, sharp teeth? What kind of machine is an elephant's trunk? What is the proboscis of an insect? Tell about the tongue of the humming-bird. How many instruments are there together in his tongue? What is said about the cat's tongue? Tell about the heron. Tell about the bird that lives on oysters. What is told about the tailor-bird? Tell about the bird that has no wings. Tell about the fish that shoots insects with water.

## CHAPTER XXV

## INSTRUMENTS OF DEFENSE AND ATTACK.

ANIMALS HAVE various instruments for defending themselves. Some have claws, some horns, some hoofs, some spurs and beaks, some powerful teeth, and some stings. These they use to defend themselves when attacked.

But man has none of these things. Why is this? It is because, as I have told you about tools, with his mind he can contrive instruments of defense, and with his hands he can use them. If men could not contrive and use such things as spears, and swords, and guns, they would stand a poor chance with some of the animals if obliged to contend with them. A lion or tiger, you know, could tear the stoutest man in pieces if he had nothing in his hands to defend himself.

It would be well if men would use the fighting instruments which they make only for defending themselves. But they often use them in attacking others, just as beasts do their weapons, and sometimes they even use their hands, and teeth, and nails in the same way that beasts do. Hands were made for useful work and innocent play; but they are often used to strike with. Teeth are given to us to eat with; but children, and even men sometimes, bite with them like an angry beast. Nails are given us for various useful purposes, but I have known children to use them in fighting as beasts do their claws and spurs.

The fighting instruments of some birds are very pow-

erful. Here are a claw and
a beak of a very cruel bird.
How fast this claw would
hold the victim, and how
would this beak tear it in
pieces! Very different are
they from the slender claws and the light beak of such
birds as the canary.

Here is a very rapacious bird, the vulture. He is on a
rock, and has under his feet a lamb which he found in
the valley below. It had perhaps wandered from the flock,

and, as it was feeding, not thinking of danger, the vulture espied it. Swiftly diving down, he caught it with his
strong claws and brought it up here. You see what a beak
he has to tear the lamb in pieces, that he may devour it.

The toucan, which you see on the opposite page, has a
larger bill than most other birds. It uses it in crushing and
tearing its food, which consists of fruits, mice, and small
birds. You see that its edges are toothed somewhat like a
saw, adapting it to tear in pieces the little animals which
this bird feeds on. But it can use its bill also for another

purpose. It is a powerful instrument of defense in fighting off the animals that attack it. The toucan makes its nest in a hole of a tree, which it digs out with its bill, if it does not readily find one already made; and there it sits, keeping off all intruders with its big beak. The mischievous monkeys are its worst enemies; but, if they get a blow from that beak, they are very careful to keep out of the way of it afterward. When the toucan sleeps, it manages to cover up this large bill with its feathers, and so it looks as if it was nothing but a great ball of feathers. There is one curious use which it makes of its bill: it uses it to trim its tail, cutting its feathers as precisely as a pair of scissors would. It takes great care in doing this, evidently thinking that it is important to its beauty. It waits till its tail is full grown before it begins to trim it.

The claws of the cat hold the rat very fast, while her long, sharp teeth tear its flesh, and pull even its bones apart. If you see a cat do this, you will get some idea of the way in which a lion or tiger tears in pieces any animal. As your cat lies quietly purring in your lap, look at her paws. The claws are all concealed, and the paw, with its cushions, seems a very gentle, peaceable thing; but wake her up and let her play with a string, and as she tries to catch it with her paw, the claws now thrust out make it look like a powerful weapon, as it really is in the eyes of rats and mice. There are muscles that work those claws when the cat's mind tells them to do it. When the claws are not thrust out these muscles are quiet, but they are ever ready to act when a message comes to them from the brain.

Did you ever think what the use is of those springy cushions in the cat's foot? They are to keep her from being jarred when she jumps down from a considerable height, as she often does. Other animals that jump have them. There is another use for these cushions. They are of assistance to animals in catching their prey. If the cat had hard, horny feet, as she went pattering around the rats and mice would take the alarm and get out of the way.

Some animals have horns which they use in attack and defense, and very powerful weapons they are in some cases. Animals that have them often defend themselves successfully against the attacks of lions, tigers, etc., that are so powerful with their teeth and claws. They gore with them. They can toss up quite a large animal into the air with them. In this animal (called the koodoo) they are nearly three feet long. You see that they have a beautiful spiral shape; indeed, the whole animal is very handsome. It lives in South Africa, in woods at the side of rivers. You might suppose that it would be rather difficult to get about among the trees and bushes with such long horns; but the koodoo manages to do this very well by throwing his head back and letting his horns rest on his shoulders.

Here is a draw-ing of a sword-fish. Its sword is made of bone, and it is so very strong that it has been known to be run through the bottom of a ship. In the British Museum there is a piece of the bottom of a ship with one of these swords run through it, and broken short off. The fish must have died at once, for such a blow must have dashed his brains out, as we say. This sword must be a powerful weapon of defense or attack in the fights of this fish with other animals.

Here is a fish that has a saw instead of a sword. The teeth, you see, are on both sides of the saw. This fish is very large, and uses this weapon with great effect in its fights with whales and other monsters of the deep. It sometimes very foolishly pushes its saw into the bottom of a ship, as the sword-fish does his sword.

There are some animals that have very singular instruments of defense. The porcupine is one. It is covered with two kinds of quills. Those of one kind are long, slender, and curved. The others are short, straight, very stout, and have a sharp point. Whenever the porcupine is chased by any animal, and finds that he can not escape by running, he stops and bristles up all his quills, as you see in the previous engraving. He then backs, so that the short, sharp quills may stick into the animal that pursues him. It has been said that he shoots his quills at any one that attacks him. But this is not so. The error came from the fact, that if any of the quills happen to be a little loose, they fall out or stick into the flesh of his adversary.

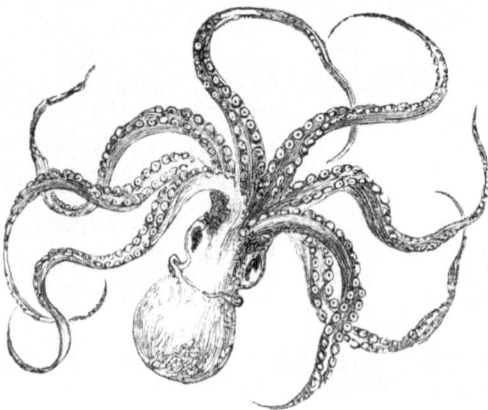

The cuttle-fish has a curious way of escaping from those fishes that attack him. He is a strangely-shaped animal, as you see. He has eight long arms, and the little spots that you see on these are suckers, with which he can stick to a rock, or can hold tightly any fish or shell that he catches. This queer-looking animal has inside of him a bag filled with a dark fluid like ink. This he uses as a means of defense in this way: if he is chased by a fish larger than he is, he empties his ink-bag in the water, and thus makes such a cloud that it blinds his pursuer, and then the cuttle-fish very easily gets out of the way.

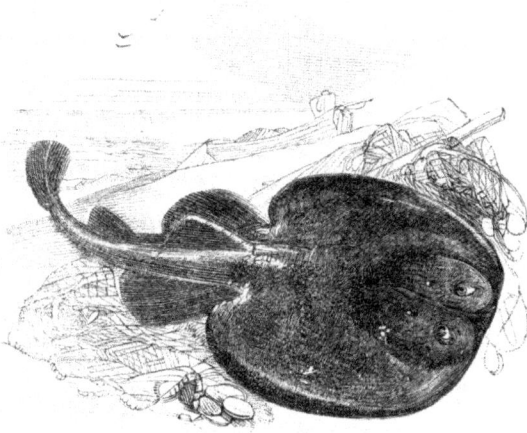

This singularly-formed fish, the torpedo, has two electrical batteries—that is, machines for making electricity or lightning; and it can give a shock when it pleases. If the fish is a large one, it can give a shock powerful enough to knock a man down. It can disable, of course, almost any fish that attempts to fight with him, and it probably uses its battery also to overcome the animals that it devours.

Here is an eel, called the electrical eel, which has the same power, and uses it for the same purposes. A sailor was once knocked down by a shock from one of these eels, and it was some time before he recovered his senses.

The different kinds of turtles, while they have no great means of attack, have most extraordinary means of defense. They have a complete suit of thick, bony armor. Most kinds of turtles can draw in their heads and limbs out of sight, and some can shut up their armor as tight as a box, and so be secure against almost any attack. This is a picture of the green turtle, which sometimes grows so large as to weigh as much as three or four men. It is found in most of the islands of the East and West Indies. Its flesh is considered a great luxury. The beautiful tortoise-shell, from which combs are made, is obtained from this armor of some kinds of turtles.

*Questions.*— What are some of the instruments of defense and attack that animals have? Why has man none of these? What is the use which men ought to make of the weapons which they contrive? How are hands, teeth, and nails often improperly used? What are the fighting instruments of birds? Tell about the vulture. Tell the different uses of the large bill of the toucan. What are the weapons of the cat? What is said about the muscles of her claws? Of what use are the cushions on her feet? Tell about the koodoo. Tell about the sword-fish and about the saw-fish. What is said about the porcupine? What about the cuttle-fish? What about the torpedo and the electrical eel? What about the turtles?

## CHAPTER XXVI

## WINGS.

BIRDS WALK upon two legs as we do; but, instead of such hands as we have, they have hands made for the purpose of lifting them up in the air. The bones in a bird's wing are very much like the bones in our arms and hands; but they make a frame-work for the feathers of the wing to spread out from. The bones that go out almost to the very end of the wing are like the bones of our fingers, only they are much longer.

A bird's wing, when it is stretched out, is a very large thing. It needs to be large to do its work well. A bird could not fly with small wings. You know that by trying very hard you jump up into the air a very little way. But see, the bird goes up very easily as high as it pleases, and does not seem to be tired. This is because its wings spread out so broadly.

The reason that birds need such large wings is this. As the bird rises by pressing upon the air, it must press on a good deal of air to do this. If it pressed upon only a little air it could not rise at all, because the air gets out of the way so easily when it is pressed upon. Swimming is flying in the water; and, as water when pressed does not get out of the way as easily as air does, the tail and fins, with which fishes swim, do not need to be as large as the wings of birds. For the same reason, hands and feet answer very well for us to swim with, though we can not fly with them. I shall tell you more particularly about this in Part Third.

Here is a very large bird, the condor. To lift such a heavy body as he has up into the air must require very large wings, and you see that he has them.

Now, to work such broad wings, the bird has very stout muscles. You know how the breast of a bird stands out. You see it here in the condor. This is because the muscles with which it works its wings are there. You can see that this is the reason when a bird is cooked. The meat, you know, is very thick on the breast-bone—thicker than in any other part of the body. If we had as large muscles on our breast-bones we should look very strange. But we do not need such large muscles to work our arms as birds do to work their wings.

A man could not fly if he had wings fixed on to his arms. It has been tried. I knew a man once to make something like wings for himself. After he had made them, he went up on to the roof of a shed to try them. He jumped off and flapped his wings, but down he came about as soon as if he had no wings, and he was so much bruised that he was not disposed to try the experiment again. Now why could he not fly? It was not for want of wings. There the wings were, and he had made them right, for he had shaped them like the wings of birds. They were large enough and light enough; the difficulty was, that the muscles of his arms were not strong enough to work them well. They were arm-muscles and not wing-muscles. A man can not be like a bird merely by having wings. He must have a bird's flying muscles, or he can not fly.

Different birds have wings of different sizes. Those that fly very far and swiftly have the largest wings. The wings of the hen are not large enough to carry her far up into the air. The most that she can do is to fly over a very high fence; and if her wings are partly cut off, or cropped, as it is called, she can not even do that. There are some birds that do not use their wings in flying. The ostrich, shown above, is a great runner. He can not fly, but his wings help him some in running.

In what way the wings act in raising birds and carrying them along I will explain to you in Part Third, when I come to tell you about the air.

How beautiful are the motions of many of the birds as they fly in the air! How easily and gracefully their wings work! See that bird as it goes up and up; and now see it as it makes a turn, and comes down so swiftly on its outstretched wings, taking a beautiful sweep off at a distance; and then up it goes again to come down, in the same way that boys do when they travel up a long hill to

slide down so swiftly on their sleds. The swallow, as he has this fine sport, is, at the same time, getting his living. As he skims along close to the ground or the water, as represented here, quick as thought he catches any unlucky fly that happens to be in his way.

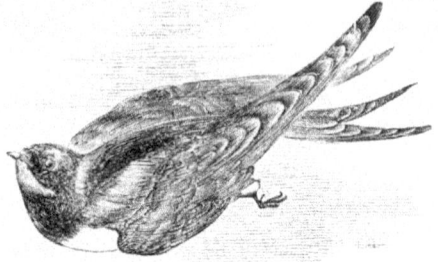

Especially beautiful are the motions of the humming-bird. See him as he stops before some flower fluttering on his wings, or as he darts with them from one flower to another. The muscles of his wings are very nimble work-men. Our muscles can make no motions as quick as these.

Did you ever examine a feather from a bird's wing to see what a curiously-made thing it is? The quill part of it is very strong, but, at the same time, light. The plume or feather part is quite strong also. It is made up of a great many very thin and delicate flat leaves, as we may call them, which are locked together curi-ously by fine teeth on their edges. If you separate them they soon come together again, and are locked as fast as ever. You can see the teeth by which they hold on to each other very well with a common microscope.

No wonder that the bat can fly so swiftly with such very broad and light wings as he has. Did you ever observe how a bat's wing is made? It is a very curious and really beautiful

thing. It is an exceedingly fine, thin skin, on a frame-work of long, slender bones. These are to it what sticks of whalebone are to an umbrella; and the wings can be folded up somewhat as an umbrella is. This is done when-ever the bat is not flying. When it is on the ground it is very awkward in its movements. It can not get a start to fly, and so it pushes itself along with its hind feet, at the same time pulling by the hooks in its wings, which it puts forward, first one and then the other, hooking them into the ground. It never likes to get upon the ground, and it takes its rest always, as you see represented on the previous page, by hanging itself up by the two hooks in its wings.

Here is a picture of the vampire bat, a native of South America, that lives by sucking the blood of ani-mals when they are asleep.

Nothing is more delicate than the wings of insects. They are like gauze; but they have a frame-work that makes them quite firm, just as leaves are firm from the ribs that are in them. Here is a drawing of the wing of a locust. But you can get no idea of the beauty of insects' wings from such draw-ings. You must exam-

ine the wings themselves. Even the wing of a common fly is very beautiful, so delicate is its structure.

The wing of the ka-tydid, as it is called, is peculiarly beautiful. Here it is. You see that it is very delicate. Its color is a light green. You see that rather thick three-cornered ridge at that part of the wing which joins the body. There is a similar ridge on the wing of the other side. In the space within this ridge there is a thin but strong membrane or skin, so that it makes a kind of drum-head. It is the rubbing together of these two drum-heads on the wings that makes the noise. It is a queer sound. There is no music in it, but the katydids seem to enjoy making it.

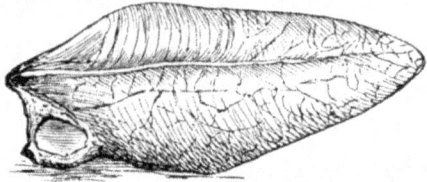

The katydid commonly makes three rubs at a time with its drum-heads. It sounds somewhat as if it said Katy-did, and from this comes its name. Sometimes there are only two rubs, and then you can fancy that it says She did or She didn't. The katydids, you know, are all quiet in the daytime, but when evening comes they are very noisy. I have often been amused to hear them as they begin just at dusk. One will begin, and perhaps say its Katy-did several times; then another, on a neighboring tree, will reply; and after a little time the whole tribe will be at work. Each one appears to rest upon it after each rubbing, and so it seems as if they answered each other from one tree and another. It is curious that you can at once stop the noise of this insect by striking the trunk of the tree on which he is with your hand.

*Questions.*— What are the bones in a bird's wing like? What is said about the size of birds' wings? What about the muscles that work them? Why can not a man fly if he makes wings for himself? What birds have the largest wings? What is said about the hen? What about the ostrich? What is said about the motions of birds in flying? What is said of the swallow? What of the humming-bird? Tell about the parts of a feather from a bird's wing. What is said about the bat's wings? What about its motions on the ground? How does it rest? What is said about the wings of insects? How does the katydid make its noise?

## CHAPTER XXVII

## COVERINGS OF ANIMALS.

THE SKIN of man is his covering. It covers up like a case all the machinery that I have told you is in his body—the bones, the muscles, the nerves, the arteries, the veins, etc. It keeps them from being injured. Besides this, how strange we should look if there were no skin to cover up these parts from view.

The skin fits very nicely all parts of the body. On the hand it is like a glove. See how well it fits. But observe that there are some places where it is quite loose and full of wrinkles. It is so between the thumb and forefinger, and around the joints of the fingers. In these places it would not do to have it fit tight, because if it did you could not move your thumb and fingers as freely as you do.

But the covering of man's body is different from that of other animals. It is, for the most part, bare skin, while most animals have either hair, or feathers, or scales, or hard plates like armor, or shells. Why is it that man has a covering that protects him so much less than animals generally are protected by their coverings? It is because he knows how to make such a covering as he needs to put on over his skin. He can suit this to the degree of heat or cold. But animals know nothing about this. No one ever saw an animal make clothes and put them on. The Creator has given to each animal such covering or clothes as it needs, ready-made. Let us look at this a little.

Animals in very cold climates need a very warm covering. They therefore have a thick fur. But animals that live in warm countries have rather thin hair instead of fur.

The elephant has very little hair, and it is only with the greatest care that he can be made to live through our cold winters. The same is true of the monkey. If these animals had a good covering of fur on their skins, the cold would not affect them in this way.

The hair of the horse is rather thin. It is not like fur; and if the horse's master is kind, he is very careful to put a good blanket on him whenever the cold makes it necessary. If he did not, the horse would get chilled and take cold. The horse is not a native of cold countries, but of such warm countries as South America and Arabia. There horses run wild, and are always in large companies or herds.

You know how thick the fur is on the cat. You can see how fine it is, and how thickly the hairs stand together, if you blow on it so as to separate the hairs. With this warm coat on her, she does not feel the cold much. You see her often in cold weather out-of-doors, with her feet gathered up under her to keep them warm. The monkey, with his thin hair, could not do so. He has to be kept in a warm place in the winter.

The covering of birds, while it is such as to keep them warm, is very light. If it were not so, they could not fly as well as they do. Feathers are so light, that, when we wish to speak of any thing as being very light, we say that it is as light as a feather. The downy feathers on the breast of birds are especially light. The feathers of the wings are different. They are made strong for the work of flying, and at the same time they are quite light. How this is done I have told you in the chapter before this.

Birds that go much into the water have an oil about their feathers which keeps them from being soaked; for this reason, a duck, when it comes out of the water, is almost as dry as before it went in. But if a hen should go into the water in the same way, she would be wet through her feathers to her skin. She was not made to go into the water, and so has neither the oily feathers nor the webbed feet which are given to the duck.

Why is it that fishes have scales? It is because they need a smooth covering in order to get along easily in the water. A covering which is rough, or which would soak in water, would be bad for them. The scales, you know, lap over one upon another, as you see here in the herring. They thus make quite a firm coat of mail, and at the same time do not hinder the bending motions of the fish. If the same covering were all in one, instead of being made up of many scales, it could not bend as easily as it does now in turning its course in the water. The scales are kept oiled, and this helps the fish to glide along swiftly. It is this that makes the fish so slippery that it is difficult to hold it in its struggles when it is first taken out of the water.

I have told you, in another chapter, about the coverings of such animals as lobsters and crabs. There is one kind of crab, called the hermit-crab, that has no covering over his tail as he has over the other parts of his body. It is therefore very liable to be injured unless it is guarded in some way. And

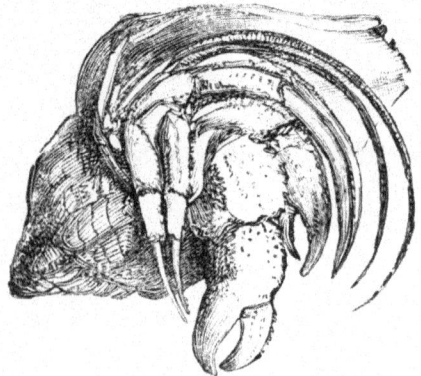

how do you think he guards it? He just puts it into some shell that he finds, as you see here, and then goes about, dragging it after him. As he grows the tail becomes too large for the shell, and as soon as he feels the shell beginning to pinch, he pulls his tail out and goes in search of another shell. It is amusing to see him try one after another till he finds one that fits well. Sometimes two of these crabs come to the same shell, and then they have a fight about it. Very foolish must a crab feel when he has driven another one off, and finds, after all, that the shell he has been fighting for does not fit his tail.

*Questions.*— What is said about our skin as a covering? What is said about its fitting well? Where are there wrinkles, and why? How is the covering of man's body different from that of other animals, and why? What is said about animals in cold climates? What about those that live in warm countries? What about the elephant, the monkey, and the horse? What about the fur of the cat? What about the covering of birds? How are the feathers of the wing different from those of the breast, and why? Why are the feathers of some birds oily? Tell about the duck and the hen. Why do fishes have scales? Why are they kept oiled? Tell about the hermit-crab.

## CHAPTER XXVIII

## BEAUTY OF THE COVERINGS OF ANIMALS.

THERE IS great variety in the coverings of insects. In some the covering is like burnished armor. The variety of colors is exceedingly great, and in many they have a splendid brilliancy. Some of the smallest insects, which most people never notice, are surpassingly beautiful when examined with the microscope. It is with them in this respect as it is with some of the smallest flowers. We know not how much beauty there is all around us in the small things that God has created till we take the microscope and look at them.

The butterflies are among the most beautiful of insects. Almost every variety of color is to be seen in them, and often many colors are seen together, arranged in the most beautiful manner. You can not have any idea of the great variety of their beauty unless you see some collection of them in cases in some museum.

You have often admired the beauty of different shells. These are the coverings of animals who lead a very quiet life in them, as I told you about the oyster. Very splendid are the colors often on the inside of these coverings, and sometimes on the outside also; and even when the outside is not at all handsome when we get the shell from the water, we

often find that clearing off the outer coating with acid, or by rubbing, will show us beautiful colors. Then, too, by grinding the shell in different parts of it, different layers are seen of different hues.

The beauty of these coverings is of no use to the animals that live in them. They have no eyes to see it. For what, then, is it intended? It is for our gratification. The Creator strews beautiful things even on the bottom of the ocean for us. If the coverings, or houses, as we may call them, of all the animals that live there were as homely as that of the oyster, they would be as useful and comfortable for them as they are now, decked with their elegant colors. So far as they are concerned, the beauty is thrown away. But men gather the shells, and, while they admire them, they see in the beauty which the Creator lavishes even

in the depths of the sea the evidence of his abounding goodness.

The variety of beauty in the coverings of birds is very great. The various colors are arranged in their plumage in every variety of manner, and there are all shades of the colors, from the most brilliant to the most delicate.

Commonly the greatest display in the plumage of birds is in the delicate and downy feathers of the breast. But the bird that you see here, the hoopoe, has its chief beauty in its crest, which is of an orange color tipped with black. It is one of the most elegant of birds.

In the peacock, a drawing of which you have on the previous page, there is a great display of colors. The animal struts about, and, lifting its tail in the air, spreads it like a fan, and seems to be very foolishly proud of its beauty. Proud people generally have something disagreeable about them, and so it is with the peacock. Its voice is so harsh and screeching that no one wants it in his neighborhood.

Birds of Paradise, as they are called, are exceedingly beautiful. There are several kinds of them. The most common kind is the one pictured here. I will give you an idea of its colors. Most of its body is a rich brown; the throat is a golden green; the head is yellow; the long, downy feathers that you see so abundant about the tail are of a soft

yellow color. This elegant bird is very careful to prevent the least speck of dirt from getting on its plumage; and when it sits on a branch of a tree it always faces the wind, so that its feathers may not be ruffled.

There is, I think, in the humming-birds more variety of color than in any other kind of birds. The colors are very brilliant, especially upon the delicate feathers of their breasts; and they are shaded in the most beautiful manner. I never saw a finer display of colors than I once saw in a collection of humming-birds in a museum in Philadelphia. Above is an engraving of a few varieties of these birds. You can see what different shapes they have. They are alike only in their long, slender bills. And when one sees a large collection of them, with all their varied forms and colors, he is struck with admiration and wonder.

Many of the furs of animals have much beauty, but there is no such great variety of color as there is in the plumage of birds. As you blow on a fine fur, and see how thickly its delicate fibres stand together, you admire its richness. Each fibre of it is in itself a beautiful thing.

We hardly know why it is that some animals that we dislike so much should have so much beauty. Worms and caterpillars are disgusting to us, and yet in many of them there is a great display of elegant colors. While writing this, I see one crawling along on my coat-sleeve with its numerous feet of curious shape. Its color is a brilliant green. On its back stand up in a row three beautiful light yellow tufts. Behind these, on a dark stripe, are two fleshy-looking round bunches, that are a most brilliant red. On its side bristle out white hairs in bundles. Its head is red, and from it extend forward dark colored but very delicate feelers, in two bundles. I suppose they are feelers, because they are shaped like the feelers of the butterfly, which you see on page 118.

Now why is it that so much beauty is given to such animals? It does not seem to be of any use. But this can not be so, for God has a use for every thing that he makes. We are to remember that he can make a thing beautiful as easily as he can make it homely. And it is just this lesson, perhaps, that he means to teach us when he clothes such creatures as worms and caterpillars in coverings of beautiful colors. It is different with us. We try to make beautiful only those things that we prize much. There are some things that it would be a foolish waste of time for us to ornament. This is because we can do but little in making things beautiful. But there is no end to God's power in the creation of beauty. He can, by the word of his power, make just as many beautiful things as he pleases.

*Questions.*— What is said about the variety of colors in insects? What is said about butterflies? What about shells? Is their beauty of any use to the animals that live in them? Why is so much beauty put in them? What is said about the variety of colors in the coverings of birds? Tell about the hoopoe. Tell about the peacock and about the birds of Paradise. What is said about humming-birds? What is said of the furs of animals? What is said about worms and caterpillars? Why is so much beauty often given to such animals?

## CHAPTER XXIX

## HOW MAN IS SUPERIOR TO ANIMALS.

YOU SEE, from what I have told you, that man can do with his hands a great variety of things that animals can not do. It has been said, therefore, by some that the hand is the great thing that makes man superior to animals. But this is not true. Of what use would the hand be if there was not a mind in the head that knew how to use it? Suppose that your cat had a hand instead of a paw, could she write with it? No; the mind in her brain does not know enough for this. And so there are a great many other things that we do with our hands which the cat would not know enough to do with hands, if she had them.

So, then, it is not the hand merely that makes you superior to a cat, but it is the mind that uses the hand. Your mind knows more than her mind does, and wants to do more things than her mind ever dreams of. Your mind, therefore, needs such an instrument as the hand to do these things with, while a paw answers very well for the cat.

God gives to every animal just such machinery as its mind can use. If it knows a great deal, that is, if it has a great deal of mind, he gives it a great deal of machinery; but if it has but little mind, he gives it but little machinery; for if he gave it much, it would not know how to work it. An oyster, as I have told you, knows but little as it lies covered up in its shell. It knows how to do only a few things, and so it has but little machinery. A dog or a cat knows a great deal more than an oyster, and therefore it has paws, claws, teeth, etc., as machinery for its mind to use. And as your mind knows so much more than that of a dog or cat, it has that wonderful machine, the hand, to do what it knows how to do.

The mind of man knows so much that it will contrive, when there are no hands, to use other things in place of them. I once saw a man who had no hands write, and do various other things very well with his toes. You know that we generally use the right hand most, making the left hand rather the helpmeet of the right. But when the right hand is lost in any way, the mind sets the left to work to learn to do as the lost one did. I once had to cut off the right arm of a very bright little girl. But her busy mind did not stop working because it had lost the best part of its machinery. In less than a fortnight I saw her sewing with her left hand, fastening her work with a pin instead of holding it as she used to do.

There is some other machinery, besides the hand, that you have which animals have not. It is the machinery that is in the face. I have told you about this before, in the chapter on the muscles. A dog, when he is pleased, looks up at you and wags his tail; but he can not laugh or even smile; neither can he frown. Why? Because there is none of the smiling, and laughing, and frowning machinery there. And so it is with other animals.

The variety of work that this machinery of expression does in the face of man is very great, as you can see if you watch the varied expressions of countenance in persons engaged in animated conversation. But there is very little variety of expression in the face of an animal. Now why is it that they have not the same muscles of expression that we have? It is for the same reason that they have not hands. The mind of man has a great many more thoughts and feelings than the mind of an animal has. It needs, therefore, more machinery to express these thoughts and feelings. The wagging of the dog's tail answers very well to express his simple feeling of pleasure; but you have so many different pleasant thoughts and feelings that you need the varied play of the muscles of the face to express them.

But some animals have certain muscles of expression in the face that we have not. They are the snarling muscles, as they are called. They draw up the upper lip on each side of the mouth in such a way as to show the long, tearing teeth. In this wolf, about to devour a lamb that he has caught, you see what a fierce and horrid expression these muscles give to the face. Now the reason that we have no such muscles is that we ought never to have snarling feelings. I have seen both men and children look very bad when they were angry; but they would have looked a great deal worse if they had snarling machinery in their faces, as wolves, and cats, and dogs have in theirs.

There is some machinery that animals have just as we do, which they can not use to do as many things as we can, because they do not know how. I will give you an example, and then you will see what I mean. Did you ever think why it is that animals can not talk? It is not because they have not the machinery for talking. Many of them have tongues, teeth, lips, etc. These are the things that we use to talk with, and yet, though they have them, and have a voice that comes out from their throats as ours does, they can not talk. Why is this? It is because they do not know how to use these parts in talking, though they do know how to use them in other things, as eating. The cow knows how to use her teeth, and lips, and tongue in eating; but if she had a mind like yours, she would use them in talking, and would not merely low.

The parrot, you know, does know how to talk, after a fashion. This particular faculty is given to it, though it is rather a stupid bird about other things. And, after all, its talking is a very awkward imitation of the speech of man; it only says what it hears people say, and that in a very bungling manner.

Though man has more machinery and can do more things than any other animal, there are some things that some animals can do better than he can. Man can climb, but he can not do it as well as a cat or a monkey. He can swim, but not as well as a fish. The frog and the grasshopper are better jumpers. The horse and the dog can run faster than he can. He can not see as far as some birds. He has but two eyes, but the fly has thousands of eyes, so that it can see in almost all directions at once. He can not smell as well as the dog, who can follow the track of his master by the scent left in his footsteps. He can mimic different sounds, but the mocking-bird can beat him at this.

But, besides all this, there are some things done by some animals that man can not do at all. He can not fly like the birds and insects. He can not go to roost like the birds. He can not walk along on the wall over his head, as the fly does with the suckers on its feet.

Each animal is fitted to do just those things that it

needs to do. For example, the monkey needs to climb to get his living, and the Creator has therefore made him so that he can climb very easily. For this purpose, instead of having two hands and two feet, as we have, he has four things shaped somewhat like hands, with which he can grasp the limbs of trees. I might give you other examples, but you can find many in the chapters on what animals use for hands, the tools of animals, and their instruments of defense and attack.

*Questions.*— What is said about the hand? In what is man superior to animals? What is said about the machinery that God gives to different animals? Tell about the man that had no hands, and about the girl that had her arm cut off. What is said about the machinery in the face? What about the variety of work that this machinery does? Why do not animals have the same muscles of expression that man has? What muscles of expression do some animals have that man has not? Why does not man have them? Why can not animals talk? What is said about the parrot? Mention some things that some animals can do better than man. Mention some things done by animals that he can not do at all. What is every animal fitted to do?

CHAPTER XXX.

## THE THINKING OF ANIMALS.

YOU SAW in the last chapter that the great superiority of man over other animals is in his mind. Let us look, now, at those things in which their minds are like his, and those things in which they differ from it.

I have already told you some things about the thinking of animals. Some of them think a great deal. They think about what they see, and hear, and feel very much as we do. I once had a cat that was born in the spring, after the snow was all gone. In the beginning of the next winter, the first snow that came was quite deep. It fell in the night. It was, of course, a new sight to my cat. When she came out in the morning, she looked at it with very curious eyes, just as we look at any thing new. I suppose that she thought how clean, and white, and pretty it was. After looking a little while, she poked the snow first with one paw and then with the other several times, to see how it felt. Then she gathered up between her paws as much as she could hold, and threw it up in the air over her head; and then she ran swiftly all around the yard, making the snow fly about like feathers wherever she went. Now, though my cat could not talk, I could see by her actions that her thoughts and feelings were very much such as children have when they play in the snow.

Animals are much like children in their sports. We notice this very often in dogs and cats. But the same thing is true of other animals. It is amusing to see porpoises playing with each other in the water. As they throw themselves up out of the water, and dive down again, they chase each other as dogs and cats do. Some birds are very lively in their sports. Insects have their sports also. The ants, industrious as they generally are, have their times for play. They run races; they wrestle; they carry each other on their backs in the same way that boys do; they run one after another, and dodge each other behind stalks of grass, as boys do behind trees and posts; they have scuffles and mock-fights together. Very busy are their minds in their little brains in these sports—as busy as your minds are in your sports.

There are some animals that you never see engaged in sports. Their thoughts seem to be always of the sober kind. You never see toads and frogs play. They always look very grave. The owl is one of the soberest-looking of animals. He looks as if he was considering something. Here is a picture of one. A man once bought an owl, supposing it to be a parrot. Some one asked him, a day or two after, if his parrot talked yet. No, said he, but he keeps up a great thinking, and I suppose he will speak his thoughts when he gets more acquainted.

Animals think a great deal in taking care of their young. What care the hen exercises over her brood of chickens! She has some of the same thoughts and feelings of love that a mother has in taking care of her child. And the bird, that has her little ones in the nest, has many thoughts about them as she goes out to gather food, and then wings her way back to put it into their open mouths.

It is interesting to watch canary-birds as they hatch and rear their young. The male bird commonly insists upon it that the female shall sit upon the nest all the time, while he takes upon himself the task of feeding her. A male canary belonging to a friend of mine was excessively particular on this point. He would not let his mate leave the nest for a moment, and if she did he would fight her till she went back. He was exceedingly busy in feeding her, and might certainly be called a good provider.

A lady gave me a very interesting account of two orioles that built their nest on a tree close by her father's house. They came regularly every year to the same spot,

and the family always knew the very day of their arrival by their joyous singing. They seemed to have the same feelings of joy that people generally do when they return to a much-loved home after a long absence. At one time one of their little ones fell from the nest. The parents manifested their concern by flying about in the most hurried, uneasy manner, and making mournful cries. The family pitied the poor birds, and the little one was carefully picked up, amid the flutterings and cries of the old birds, and was replaced in the nest. And now the joy of the parent birds over their restored one was expressed by a long and merry peal of song, as they sat perched on the branch close by their little nestlings. At length one of these orioles died, and the other left the nest and never more returned.

See that spider on his web. He is watching for flies. The mind in his little brain thinks of every fly that comes buzzing along, and is anxious that it should get its legs entangled in the snares that he has woven. How glad he feels when he sees one caught by these snares! And if he thinks that they are not strong enough to hold the fly, he runs and quickly weaves some more threads about him. In the same way do all animals that catch their prey think very busily while they are doing it.

Animals think much in building their dwellings. The bird searches for what it can use in building its nest, and in doing this it thinks. The beavers think as they build their dams and their houses. They think in getting their materials, and also in arranging them, and in plastering them together with mud.

Some spiders build houses that you would think must have been made by some thinking creature. They have no brain, but small, nervous threads with here and there

knots which seem to answer as little brains. You have learned something of this in Chapter XVIII.

How we see, occasionally, creatures doing more intelligent things than we expect them to do, if we judge them according to the amount of brain they have. We know that a man may do things that a monkey cannot: and we see that man has a larger brain ; the largest of all. We see, also, that a monkey can do more intelligent things than a cat or a cow, because his brain is larger in proportion ; and so through the whole animal creation.

There are now and again creatures exhibiting strange faculties ; they do things that one would think could only be done by man. We cannot yet explain this, but we may admire these things, and bear in mind that the Creator has designed all things well.

A kind of tarantula, the spider whose bite is poisonous, builds its house in a wonderful manner. It first digs a hole in the ground, and then lines it by spinning a pure white satin-like silk over the interior, making the sides one continuous tube of silk. When you come to study the insects, you will learn how this spinning is done. When the underground room or cellar is finished, the spider proceeds to pile up bits of wood, and he places them just as boys build log houses, by laying them at right angles on each other. You will see a picture of this spider's nest on the preceding page.

Persons have watched these spiders closely, at work. Does it not seem too wonderful to be true; but they have been seen. The spaces between the logs, or sticks, he fills with plaster, made up by wetting the earth by his mouth.

The silk he spins for lining is as good as that made from the silk-worm. A spider that is very common in Florida weaves its net across bushes, and

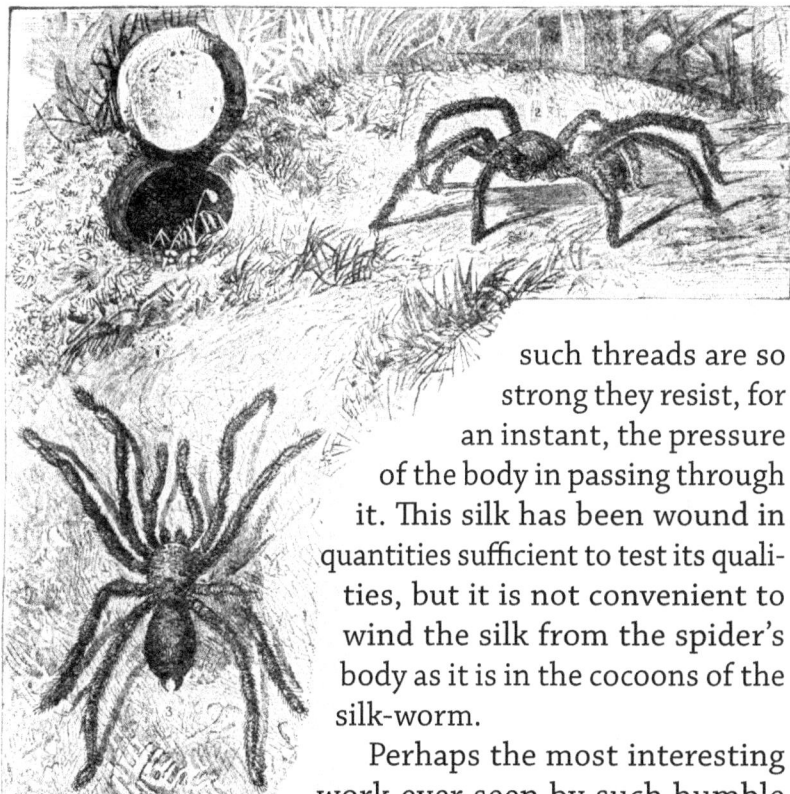

such threads are so strong they resist, for an instant, the pressure of the body in passing through it. This silk has been wound in quantities sufficient to test its qualities, but it is not convenient to wind the silk from the spider's body as it is in the cocoons of the silk-worm.

Perhaps the most interesting work ever seen by such humble creatures is the nest of the trapdoor spiders. These nests are entirely underground, and open on the surface, always on a slight incline. It is impossible to distinguish the nest until the door is opened. Then it is seen that the opening is fitted with a stopper so tightly closed there is no line to show where it fits. The nest is about eight inches deep, and is a straight tube an inch and a half in diameter inside. This tube is lined completely with beautiful satin-silk. The stopper or trap-door is made of mud, and lined with silk, which is connected with the silk of the interior by a narrow bar, which forms a hinge. It all looks like the hand of man. We see what design there is in placing the nests all on a side hill. The spider takes advantage of this, and puts his hinge on the cover and tube on the highest point, so that the cover will always surely fall down and shut him in when he retreats. If you try to pry open his door he seizes hold of the inner side of it and pulls with all his might, only giving up when the tube is broken. The best security is from the chances of the door escaping detection entirely, for one cannot see where the sharp lines are that form the borders. The grass, too, aids in concealing it. There are some that have a second tube, built underground, an offshoot from the first; in this is a second valve, or trap-door, behind which the spider retreats when pushed beyond the first entrance. This kind of spider reminds us of some warrior or chief, who has a castle to live in and defend. These houses all have a small hole at the bottom, through which any moisture escapes. The trap-doors or stoppers to these tubes are so circular that they look as if punched out by a perfectly circular steel implement.

On the Florida Reef lives, among many another kind of worm, one that builds up a house much as the tarantula builds. It lives on the flats, in shallow water, where one can examine it very closely. It belongs to an order of worms called *Annelids*. It has no long limbs, and nothing but soft tentacles to work with, which are around the mouth. With these soft tentacles the worm reaches forth and selects certain bits of debris and builds up a tube, several inches in length. The bottom of the shallow flats, where these house-building worms are seen, is mostly made up of bits of coral and little limestone leaves of corallines, or seaweeds that have a lime skeleton or framework within the green portion. When these seaweeds die, the green and vegetable portion washes away, and leaves a frame of lime, made up of little heart-shaped blocks. The wonderful part of this worm's work is, that it selects these little tiles of lime, and builds up its tube exclusively of them. The little tiles are flat, and they are placed one upon the other just as a faced-stone wall is built. During the construction of this wall the creature introduces here and there bits of green algae, that hang down and conceal somewhat the work; and this produces a protection, from its resemblance to the surrounding seaweeds, thus cheating the hungry fishes that are looking around for a bite. Still more wonderful is the fact that the creature tops off his tube by constructing a cover. A bit of shell hinged at one point by some glue-like substance, which he also uses for lining his tube, is covered with green seaweeds.

It is singular that a spider should exercise so much intelligence (seemingly), but here is a worm, quite low in the scale of life, doing what we expect to see done only by the highest animals. Nature has given these lowly creatures this faculty of deception, which allows them to place weeds upon their structures, to resemble the surrounding growth.

*Questions.*— What is said about the thinking of animals? What is told about a cat? What is said about the sports of animals? Tell about the ants. Tell about the owl. What is said about animals taking care of their young? Tell about the canary-bird. Tell about the orioles. What is said about the spider? What is said about animals building their dwellings? What of the house-building spiders? Have they a brain? What have they instead? What do they do that is strange? What animal has the largest brain? Why does a monkey do more intelligent things than a cat? What is a tarantula? What of its bite? Does it build a house? How is it built? What does the spider build on the top of the cellar? How does he fill up the spaces left between the logs or sticks? What is the nature of the silk? What of the spider in Florida? What of the trap-door spiders? Describe the nest. How is it lined? What does it look like? Why are the nests all placed on an incline or side hill? What happens when you try to pry open a nest? What of the worm on the Florida Reef? To what order does the worm belong? What does it work with? What is the nature of the flats on which the worm builds? What kind of material does the worm use in building? Describe the nature of the corallines. What does the worm do to deceive? What does the worm do to line his tube? What is strange about this house-building by a worm?

## CHAPTER XXXI

## MORE ABOUT THE THINKING OF ANIMALS.

A S ANIMALS think, they learn. Some learn more than others. The dog learns a good deal; so do the monkey and the elephant. Some are good at learning some particular things. The parrot learns to mimic talking, though it is quite stupid about some other things. The mockingbird learns to imitate a great many different sounds. The shepherd's dog, seen here, though he does not know as much about most things as dogs of some other kinds, understands particularly well how to take care of sheep. If he is trained to this business, he will show great skill in doing it. James Hogg, a Scotch poet, commonly called the Ettrick Shepherd, relates many wonderful anecdotes of his dog, whom he called Sirrah. He says that one night a large flock of lambs got out from their fold and ran away among the hills. When the shepherd said, "Sirrah, they're a' awa'!" the dog dashed off after them, and was soon out of sight. The shepherd also, and his man, started off in pursuit. They searched all night, but could find nothing of the dog or the lambs; but in the morning they espied Sirrah standing guard at the mouth of a gorge, or narrow pass, and anxiously looking for his master to come.

He had succeeded in finding all the scattered lambs, and here they were in this gorge, into which he had driven them. It is told of another dog of this kind that he would pick out any stray sheep from the midst of a whole flock, and drive it back to the flock to which it belonged. This dog was once observed trying to drive a flock over a bridge which they were afraid to cross. He managed very well, and at length succeeded in getting them over. It was amusing to see how he did it. At one moment he was driving up some of the scattered ones, and the next he was among the foremost, urging them forward. After a while he made some of the foremost pass over, and then the whole flock followed.

Though animals think and learn, they do not have much originality. They always do things very much in the same way. They do not keep contriving some new ways of doing things as men do. Each kind of bird has its own way of building a nest, and it is always the same way. The robins build their nests now just as they did hundreds of years ago. The moles build their tunneled habitations under ground year after year after the plan that you see on page 107. And so of other animals. They have no new fashions, and learn none from each other. But men, you know, are always contriving new ways of building houses, or learning them from other men.

Many of the things that animals know how to do they seem to know either without learning, or without learning in the same way that we learn. They are said to do such things by instinct; but what instinct really is no one can tell. It is by this instinct that birds build their nests, and bees their honeycombs, and beavers their dams and huts. If these things were all contrived and thought out just as men contrive houses, there would be some changes in the fashions of them, and some improvements. Nearly all that we know about this instinct is that some very nice things are done by it, without much thinking being mixed up with it.

This want of thinking sometimes leads to some queer mistakes. If you put a duck's eggs in a hen's nest, she will sit on them as if they were her own eggs, and after the ducks are hatched she will take care of them, not seeming to know that, they are not chickens. One would suppose that she would know, because they look so different from chickens, and have bills so unlike theirs. But she does not seem to think of this. And it is amusing to see her after the ducks get large enough to go into the water. Off they run, and plunge in, and swim about, while the old hen stands by the water, greatly alarmed lest they should be drowned. She does not understand it; she does not know that ducklings have an instinct different from chickens.

So, too, if the hen has rounded pieces of chalk put in her nest, she will sit on them as if they were real eggs. Her instinct makes her sit; but if she had much reason she would not sit on pieces of chalk. If she thought much, she would find out what they were and quit her nest.

I have mentioned the building instinct of the beavers. An English gentleman caught a young one and put him at first in a cage. After a while he let him out in a room where there was a great variety of things. As soon as he was let out he began to exercise his building instinct. He gathered together whatever he could find, brushes, baskets, boots, clothes, sticks, bits of coal, etc., and arranged them as if to build a dam. Now, if he had his wits about him, as we should say, he would have thought that there was no use in building a dam where there is no water. It is from such mistakes as these that I have mentioned that the instinct of animals is said to be blind.

It is plain that, while animals learn about things by their senses as we do, they do not think nearly as much about what they learn, and this is one reason that they do not know as much as we do. Even the wisest of them, as the elephant and the dog, do not think over what they see and hear very much.

But this is not all. There are some things that we understand about which animals know nothing. They know nothing about what happened before they were born, or what happens now in their lifetime away from them in other places. They know nothing about what is to happen. They know nothing about God and another world. You can not teach them any thing about any such subjects. The reason is, that while their minds are like ours in some things, they are different in other things.

You can see this great difference between your minds and the minds of animals in one thing. You never would think of telling a story to a dog or a cat as you would to a child, for you know that it would not be understood.

The minds of animals are so much unlike ours that they do not know the difference between right and wrong. Some suppose that a dog will not do certain things because he knows that it is wrong to do them. But this is not so. He is afraid to do what he would be whipped for. If he sees a piece of meat on a table, he will not take it simply because he knows his master would not like it, and not because he knows that it is wrong to steal.

I have told you that the mind uses the brain in thinking. Now some learned men have been so foolish as to say that it is the brain itself that does the thinking, just as if our brains, and the brains of all animals, are only so many machines that make thoughts and feelings. Of course, such men do not believe that, after death, the mind or soul of man leaves the body and lives separate from it. They believe that when the body dies there is an end to every thing. But God has told us differently from this in his word, and he knows all about such things; and those that pretend to know that it is not as God says it is, show great wickedness as well as folly.

*Questions.*— What is said about the learning of animals? Tell about the shepherd's dog. What is said about the contrivance of animals? Why do they have no new fashions? What is said about instinct? Tell about the hen's hatching duck's eggs. Tell about her sitting on pieces of chalk. What is told about the beaver? What is one reason that animals do not know as much as we do? What things do they know nothing about? Do they know the difference between right and wrong? What is said about the notions of some learned men?

## WHAT SLEEP IS FOR.

ALL ANIMALS have their times for sleeping. It would not do for their minds to use the machinery of the body all the time; if they did, the machinery would soon wear out. The brain, and nerves, and muscles, etc., are all repaired during sleep, so that they may be ready for use again.

When you feel tired, it is because your mind has worn the machinery of the body by using it. Now, when you lie down and sleep, the muscles stop working; no messages pass through the nerves, and the brain is at rest, because the mind pretty much stops thinking. But all this time that you sleep the blood keeps circulating, and the breathing goes on. What is this for? It is that the repairing of the machinery may be done, so as to get the brain, and nerves, and muscles ready for the work and the play of to-morrow. The repairing, you know, is all done with the blood. This is the material for repairing as well as for building, and therefore it must be circulating every where while you are asleep, and the breathing must go on to keep the blood in good order.

The repairing of the body is going on all the time while you are awake as well as when you are asleep. But it goes on more briskly when the machinery is not in use than when it is. So we may say that when you are asleep the machinery is lying by for a full repair.

The same is true of the building of the body. More of it is done when you are asleep than when you are awake. You are growing all the time, but you grow most when you are asleep. And it is because the child is growing that he needs more sleep than the adult does. The baby is growing very fast, and so he sleeps a great deal of his time in the day as well as in the night.

The night is given to us as the time to sleep. Then it is dark and still, and we can go to sleep easily. Most animals sleep through the night. You remember that I told you, in Chapter X., Part First, how still the garden becomes as evening comes on. The flies, and bees, and bugs, and birds have gone to rest, to get repaired for the next day; so, too, have the larger animals. But it is curious that some animals are busy in the night, and take their sleep in the day. It is so with the owl and the bat. The katydid, you know, does not begin its noise till evening. I suppose that it sleeps in the daytime.

Those people that stay up late at night, and do not get up early in the morning, make a great mistake. They do not take the right time for sleeping. They ought not to turn night into day, as bats, and owls, and katydids do, for they are not made for it.

When you are tired and need sleep, the trouble is not merely in the muscles. If it was, then keeping still merely, without sleeping, would answer. But the brain and nerves need repairing as well as the muscles. But as long as you are seeing, and hearing, and feeling, the nerves are kept too busy to be repaired well; and as long as your mind keeps thinking, the brain does not get thoroughly repaired. So, then, merely keeping still will only repair the muscles; and sleep is needed to repair the brain and the nerves.

You know that when you dream very much you are not as much refreshed as when you sleep soundly. What is the reason? It is because that when you dream the mind is not wholly at rest, and works the brain, so that it is not thoroughly repaired.

There is another kind of sleep into which some animals go. It is a very long sleep. It lasts all winter. Great numbers of such animals as frogs, bats, flies, and spiders, go into by-places in the fall to sleep till spring comes. Many of the birds do this.

It is a deeper sleep than that which animals go into at night. It is a different kind of sleep. In the sleep at night the blood keeps moving, and the animal breathes; but in this winter sleep there is no breathing, and the blood stops circulating. All is as still as death. But there is life there, just as I told you, in Part First, there is life in the seed, and in the trees that look so dead in winter. It is life asleep. The warmth of spring wakes up again the life in these animals, as it does the life in the trees. The blood then begins to circulate in them, as the sap does in the trees, and they come out from their hiding-places.

I have said that this sleep which some animals go into lasts through the winter. It may be made to last longer than this. Some frogs were once kept in this winter sleep for over three years in an ice-house; and then, on being brought out into the warm air, revived and hopped about as lively as ever. We do not know how much longer they might have been kept in this sleep. You remember that in Part First, Chapter XV., I told you about some seeds in which the life was asleep many hundred years. And it may be that the life might be kept asleep in frogs and other animals as long as this by steady cold. A toad was found lately in the middle of a tree fast asleep. How he came there was not known, but the wood had kept growing year after year, and as there were 67 rings outside of the toad, it was clear that he had been there 67 years. A long sleep it was, but he soon woke up and hopped about like other toads.

There are some kinds of animals that crawl into winter quarters in whom life is not wholly asleep. The blood moves a little, and they once in a while take a breath; and, besides, they now and then, when the weather is quite warm, wake up enough to eat a little. Now it is curious that such animals always lay up something to eat right alongside of them when they go into their winter sleeping-places. But those who do not wake up at all do not lay up any food, for it would not be used if they did lay it up. They are governed by instinct in this matter.

The field-mouse lays up at its side nuts and grain when it goes into its winter quarters, and when it is partly waked up by a warm day, eats a little of his store. The bat does not lay up any thing, although he wakes up when it is warm. He does not need to lay up any thing, because the warmth that wakes him up wakes up also gnats and insects on which he lives. He catches some of these, and then, as he finds himself going to sleep again, he hangs himself up by his hooks as before. The marmot or woodchuck does not wake up at all, but he always lays up some dried grass in his hole. What is this for? He feeds on it when he first wakes up in the spring, to get a little strength before he comes out from his hole.

How much life, then, is asleep in the winter in animals as well as in plants! And how busy is life in its waking in the spring! While the roots and seeds in the ground send up their shoots, and the sap again circulates in the trees and shrubs, and the buds swell, multitudes of animals are crawling out of their winter hiding-places into the warm, balmy air. And when the leaves are fully out, and the flowers abound, the earth swarms with the busy insects, and birds, and creeping things, of which we saw none during the winter.

Some of the birds that we see in the spring have not been asleep during the cold weather, but have spent their winter at the South, and have now winged their way back to spend their summer with us. They go back and forth in this way every year, guided by that wonderful and mysterious thing, instinct. How this makes them take their flight at the right time, and in the right direction, we do not understand.

*Questions.*— Why do animals need sleep? Why do you feel tired after work, or play, or study? Why does the blood circulate and the breathing go on in sleep? When is most of the repairing of the body done? How is it with its growth? What is said about night as the time for sleep? Mention some animals that sleep in the day and are awake in the night. What is said about people that turn night into day? Why would not merely keeping the body still, without sleeping, answer for our rest? What is said about dreaming? What is said of the winter sleep of some animals? Tell about the frogs and the toad. Why do some animals take food into their winter sleeping-places? Tell about the field-mouse, the bat, and the marmot. What is said about the waking up of life in the spring in animals and in plants? What is said about the birds?

## HYGIENE.

IN SOME of the chapters you have learned how our bodies are made, and how they are kept alive; you have seen how much, like machinery the different parts of the body are. To take good care of these different parts of our body is what we are expected to do; it is reasonable for us to do so, because we suffer if we do not. But it is wicked, also, if we neglect such duties, for the good Father has given us life and the faculties for its preservation to good old age. The knowledge and care that we use in such duties is called hygiene.

We do wrong if we do not carefully preserve our natural good health by the use of faculties we have. One of the first and the simplest rules of health, or hygiene, we should heed is, be cleanly. No respectable person will long be otherwise.

In your studies in physiology you find that the skin is full of pores that reach down to glands or little sacs. These give out a fluid from the blood we call perspiration. If one is not cleanly, by frequent washing, the little pores become filled up, the moisture hardens, and the free circulation is stopped ; and this is liable to be injurious to health.

Hygiene, then, teaches us to get a knowledge of all we can of the machinery of our bodies, and honestly to use it always when necessary for the preservation of our health. A very necessary thing to do is to prevent a sudden check of perspiration, as many very dangerous diseases come right from such carelessness. The feet should always be kept warm, and the shoes and stockings well and quickly dried, when wet. Sitting in a draft of air, in coaches, cars, and many other places, often causes serious diseases. We should dress warmly, but so as to preserve a uniform, comfortable condition, in doors or out. We should avoid being chilled, and, if so exposed, should get warm as soon as possible; especially care should be taken to heat the feet well after such exposure.

Hygiene teaches us to preserve health by eating and drinking what is known to be wholesome for us. Our parents are good teachers in such things; they usually give what is for the best, and advise against what is wrong and hurtful. Therefore it is wise and best for the young to observe, carefully and strictly, the advice of their parents.

It would seem that when you are old enough to notice the disgusting looks of a drunkard, and see the dreadful sufferings he brings on his family, his wife, and his children-their loss of home, and sufferings from starvation-all this, one would think, should caution us against the use of intoxicating drinks for pleasure. Horrible beyond measure is the result to the drinker, if he continues. It is dangerous to meddle with it for a moment, and it is much the best to have nothing at all to do with it, excepting through a prescription of a doctor.

Many people find that it makes them want more, the more they drink, and, like all that is evil, it carries them onward to a bad end. One very bad result is, to those who become regular drinkers, the loss of moral faculty. Such persons are not so truthful, and there is little to hold them from doing much that is evil. Such are easily led astray. This is a sad thing to reflect on, but it is too true. Then, let our young folks shun such evil things.

There are some curious facts that show that alcoholic drinks are not even so valuable for a medicine as was once thought. Those who brave the intense cold of the arctic regions find that the use of much alcoholic liquor is no help to them, and survive, when those who depend on daily drinks suffer, and die even. Men who have all their faculties in a natural condition find that they bear the heat and cold of the tropic and arctic regions much better and more safely than those who depend upon spirits to help them. The latter, in cases of great emergency, are known to lose courage quickly. Men undergoing training for violent exercises do not use alcoholic liquors at such times, even if they do at others, knowing that alcohol really weakens the muscles, the stimulus of a drink soon passing off, and leaving a corresponding want behind. People who habitually use liquors are not so likely to survive serious illness. Our young folks will, then, abstain from such unreasonable courses, and lead healthy and godly lives.

There are many other articles besides spirits, called narcotics, which are such deadly poisons, one would think it unnecessary to caution people against their use. Leave them all to your doctor, and do not dare to use any without his advice, for they are dangerous. They soon beget an appetite, as rum does, which brings ruin in every form. The stomach is disturbed, and many ailments are produced that you would shudder to know about.

Tobacco. This is another, and a very useless, article to shun. Smoking and chewing tobacco are idle habits at best, arid cannot but be bad in some way. One would suppose that the nauseating effects of a trial at smoking or chewing would prevent our boys from further trials; but it seems manly, they think. Oh, no, it is not manly; leave them alone. There are many reasons why smoking and chewing are very undesirable, besides being an injury to health. Our comfortable homes are polluted by the stale tobacco smoke; the floors are sometimes not free from the vile juices. No household can be sweet and clean where tobacco is used to considerable extent.

The worst thing that happens to those who smoke to excess, and it is usually those who are sedentary in occupation that are affected, is a general paralysis, first felt in vertigo, confusion of the mind, and tingling of the finger nerves. These symptoms should prompt a complete abandonment of tobacco.

Cigarettes are thought to be very injurious; perhaps the paper is most irritating. Smoking tobacco induces a depression of spirits that calls for stimulants. In that respect it is doubly dangerous.

*Questions.*—*What* is hygiene? Why should we first of all take good care of our body? What is the simplest rule of hygiene? Describe the pores of the skin? What fluid is given out from them? From what does the perspiration come? What happens if the pores of the skin become stopped? What does hygiene teach? What is another very important thing to do? What about the feet? Why should we avoid being in a draft of air? How should we dress? What should we do after exposure to wet? What further does hygiene teach? Who are the good teachers in such things? Why should we let spirituous liquors entirely alone? What happens to many who drink habitually? What is one very bad result mentioned? What happens in such cases? What do some curious facts show? What about men who have all faculties in a natural condition in the tropics and arctic zones? How do men that train for violent exercise do? What effect does alcoholic liquors have on the muscles? What else happens to people that habitually drink much alcoholic liquor? What about other stimulants, narcotics, etc. ? What is best to do with them ? What effects are seen from the use of narcotics? What about tobacco? What would one suppose concerning the use of tobacco ? What do boys think of the habit of smoking? What do you think of it? Why are the habits of smoking and chewing very undesirable as well as hurtful? What is sometimes the effect of the use of tobacco on the brain? What should be done in such a case? Why are cigarettes more hurtful ?

## CHAPTER XXXIII

## WHAT TO DO IN AN EMERGENCY.

THERE ARE many things we may do for the relief of people who are in danger. If you observe the simple rules for the recovery of persons rescued from drowning, you do what a doctor cannot do, unless he comes in time. One may have been under water some minutes-from fifteen to thirty-and all appearance of life gone. Such a person may not live if let alone; but you are, happily, at hand, and immediately turn his face downward, and heels and lower body upward, to let out the water from his month. Yon quickly, but gently, press once against his ribs with a band on each side of his chest ; then you blow forcibly into his mouth, with his nostrils closed, and again you press his chest, and again blow into his mouth to inflate his lungs. You do all this to make him breathe. If you have anything at hand that will irritate his nose, it is valuable—snuff, or even tickling the nose with a straw, is good; and the result is, sometimes, that the person will be convulsed in those parts, and sneeze—a most happy occurrence, for then the lungs are brought into action. Heat, by any means, is valuable now-warm clothes, etc.; but this is of little value before the all-necessary action of the lungs.

A most memorable instance of resuscitation occurred to us in the case of a fisherman who was taken ashore after being, at least, thirty minutes under water. All means seemed to fail, even shocks from a galvanic battery. A bottle of tincture of cayenne pepper was at hand, and a few drops of that turned into the nose produced instant sneezing, which inflated the lungs sufficiently to continue the functions of life.

This is recorded as an instance of what may be done, even at the last extremity. A prompt application of a few simple remedies will often save life, when, if yon wait for a doctor, all is lost.

Boys and girls should learn to swim; there ought to be no exception to this. One increases his chances for life many times by being able to swim. Any one may learn by taking into the water with him a board to rest upon; but a flat rubber bag is best. Salt water, of considerable depth, is the best for learners.

Fainting is often treated wrongly. Most persons know what fainting is, and it is desirable that all should know. When a person faints, the simplest remedy is to lay them down horizontally; water, or rubbing, or anything else, even ammonia, is of little account compared to the effect of lowering the head.

Fainting is simply a temporary loss of the usual volume of blood in the head-a slight and usually harmless occurrence that requires first the reclined position, and then fresh air. But persons in a faint should not be kept upright, even if they have no fresh air or other restoratives.

All is of little importance beyond the relief of the brain by a recumbent posture. Therefore, in case of fainting in a close room, as is often the case, as in a theatre or lecture-room, the person should be laid upon the seat, or floor, even, rather than be carried out at the risk of the head remaining upright.

It should be the duty of young folks to learn physiology and the nature of some few simple and common ailments, that they may readily lend aid in emergencies. They should certainly learn to distinguish the difference between fainting and "fits," as they are called. The latter are known at once by the twitching of the face and body, and the frothing at the month. Persons thus affected should be placed in a nearly upright position, as it often happens the illness is apoplectic, a" rush of blood to the head," so to speak, and requires just the opposite treatment to that used in fainting. Cold water, in either case, applied to the head freely, is very useful as a remedy.

These are among the more important emergencies in which all, as intelligent citizens and Christians, should be ready to give aid. No young person should allow himself to be in the least ignorant of them. Let it, then, be a duty to know all about the subject, and be prepared to help yourself or any one you may meet in distress.

There are some other things you will learn from a study of anatomy and physiology. Yon should know what to do if you cut your own or another's limbs or body. If an artery is cut you should be ready with your knowledge that the blood is coming from the heart, in all directions, towards the extremities to the fingers, to the toes, to the head. Therefore you will; if an artery is cut in your head or neck, press on the part that is between the cut and the heart. You will also, if the hand or arm is cut in the course of an artery, tie a bandage on *above* the cut, or press your finger on the great vein above where it is bleeding. So with the feet and legs; the great artery that you may feel right under the knee, or up in the inside of the thigh, must be pressed upon tightly if the cut is below; and this is to be done until you are relieved by a doctor. Many a person has had his life saved by some bright one that had learned how to do these simple things. How much a duty it is, then, to learn!

*Questions.*— What would you do if a person had been to all appearances drowned? Why do you blow into his mouth and press on his chest alternately? what about irritating his nose? What is all-important to be done first? What about heat? How long a time is it stated a man remained nuder water, and yet was restored? By what was he restored? What effect did the tincture have on the body? Why is this example mentioned? Why should you not wait for a doctor? Why should boys and girls learn to swim? How may one learn to swim? What water is most favorable? What is fainting? Is it comparatively harmless? What position is necessary to restore a person in a faint? Which is most important, the horizontal position or fresh air? What would you do in a close room when one faints? What is the real duty of young folks in this particular? What is important to distinguish? What difference is there? What would you do if you saw one in a fit? Why is it more proper to raise the head of one in a fit? What handy thing is useful in any case? Why is it our duty to know how to give aid in emergencies of this kind? What about anatomy and physiology? What would you do, if an artery were cut on the head or neck, to check the flow of blood? What if the hand or forearm is cut? What if the foot or leg? Why would you press on the artery, if yon can find it, or the part near it, in such eases? Is it not our duty to know how to do these things?

THE END